# DISCOVERING THE BIBLE
# DAVID
## and
# GOLIATH
### *and* other Old Testament stories

RETOLD BY *Victoria Parker*

CONSULTANT *Janet Dyson*

DISCOVERING THE BIBLE

# DAVID
## and
# GOLIATH
### <u>and</u> other Old Testament stories

RETOLD BY *Victoria Parker* ✣ CONSULTANT *Janet Dyson*

Published by Anness Publishing Ltd,
Blaby Road, Wigston, Leicestershire LE18 4SE

Email: info@anness.com

Web: www.annesspublishing.com

Anness Publishing has a new picture agency outlet for images
for publishing, promotions or advertising. Please visit our
website www.practicalpictures.com for more information.

Publisher: Joanna Lorenz
Managing Editor: Gilly Cameron Cooper
Senior Editor: Lisa Miles
Produced by Miles Kelly Publishing Limited
Editorial Director: Paula Borton
Art Director: Clare Sleven
Project Editor: Neil de Cort
Editorial Assistant: Simon Nevill
Designer: Jill Mumford
Information Author: Kamini Khanduri
Artwork Commissioning: Suzanne Grant and Lynne French
Picture Research: Kate Miles and Janice Bracken
Lesley Cartlidge and Liberty Mella
Copy Editing: AD Publishing Services
Indexing: Janet De Saulles
Design Consultant and Cover Design: Sarah Ponder
Education Consultant: Janet Dyson

Miles Kelly Publishing Limited
11 Bardfield Centre, Great Bardfield, Essex CM7 4SL

ETHICAL TRADING POLICY
Because of our ongoing ecological investment programme, you, as our
customer, can have the pleasure and reassurance of knowing that a tree is
being cultivated on your behalf to naturally replace the materials used to
make the book you are holding. For further information about this
scheme, go to www.annesspublishing.com/trees

PUBLISHER'S NOTE
Although the advice and information in this book are believed to be
accurate and true at the time of going to press, neither the authors nor
the publisher can accept any legal responsibility or liability for any errors
or omissions that may have been made.

PHOTOGRAPHIC CREDITS
6 (B/L) Sonia Halliday Photographs.
11 (B/R) Richard T. Nowitz/ CORBIS
32 (B/R) Erich Lessing/ AKG London.
40 (B/R) H Fenn/ Mary Evans Picture Library.
44 (B/L) John Spaull/ Panos Pictures.
All other images from the Miles Kelly Archive.

The Publishers would like to thank the following artists who have
contributed to this book:
Inklink Studio (Virgil Pomfret Agency): Simone Boni, Francesco
Petracchi, Lucia Mattioli, Theo Caneschi, Federico Ferniani,
Alain Bressan, Loredano Ugolini, Alessandro Rabatti,
Lorenzo Pieri, Luigi Critone
Also: Vanessa Card, Rob Sheffield, Sally Holmes, Terry Riley, Terry Gabbey,
Sue Stitt, Peter Sarson, John James, Mike White, Wayne Ford
Maps by Martin Sanders

# Contents

# Introduction

HERE you can read about the Israelites' battles amongst themselves and with their neighbours, and charts the rises and falls of their faith in God. It covers the period of time from Samuel through the reigns of the first kings of Israel, to the division of the kingdom into two nations, Israel and Judah.

The story starts with the story of Samuel, who, brought up by Eli the High Priest, was called by God as a prophet at an early age. He went on to rule Israel as a Judge, a ruler of Israel called by God. Under Samuel's leadership the Israelites' faith in God was restored. When he got older the people asked him for a king, so God instructed Samuel to anoint Saul the first king of Israel.

Saul was very popular with his people and successful in war, but things soon started to go wrong. Saul disobeyed God several times. He was eventually punished when God rejected him as king, and Samuel anointed a shepherd boy called David as Israel's next king. David became very popular after killing the Philistine giant Goliath. Saul became so jealous that he tried to kill David who escaped to safety in the wilderness where he lived for many years. He only returned to Israel after Saul and his four sons died during a battle with the Philistines.

After Saul's death, David eventually became king over all Israel. He captured the city of Jerusalem and made it his capital, setting up the tabernacle there, and bringing back the ark. It was David who wanted to build a temple, a permanent home for the Ark of the Covenant containing their sacred laws, but God decreed this would be done by the next king, David's son, Solomon.

**Jerusalem**
David decided when he became king that he wanted Jerusalem as his capital. It is now known as the "City of David".

When Solomon took the throne on David's death, his main aim was to maintain the peace that his father had achieved. Solomon concentrated on developing trading links with his neighbours, and he channelled his energies into huge building projects, the most important of which was the temple in Jerusalem. As part of his plan to forge links with his neighbours, he married many foreign women, but his wives reintroduced pagan gods into Israel and Solomon joined them in their worship. God's punishment to Solomon was to split the kingdom in two, and only two of the 12 tribes were given to his son. The other ten crowned a government official called Jeroboam as their ruler.

Until the era of the kings, the Israelites had been led by Judges or priests. The first king, Saul, was requested by the people. Samuel tried to persuade them to be content to worship God as their king, but they wanted to be like their neighbours. God gave His consent, but warned that a king would make demands on his people, and a king would not be as forgiving as God had been.

The king's role developed as it passed from Saul, to David, to Solomon. Saul was a fine warrior king but never quite established his position as religious leader – it was Samuel who performed this role during his lifetime. David was very successful, he was in many ways the ideal king. He established Israel as a nation state and founded a dynasty that lasted for over 400 years. Because he had been involved in warfare he was not allowed to build a temple – that role fell to Solomon who was wise, peaceful, but was not, and could never be, perfect.

David is very significant in Jewish history. The Star of David is the symbol of Judaism and features on the Israeli flag today. After David's death, the Jews hoped for a Messiah (an "anointed one"), a righteous leader descended from David, who would reunite the tribes of Israel and restore Israel's position in the world. The message of the New Testament is that this hope was fulfilled in Jesus Christ, and the lineage from David to Jesus is traced at the beginning of Matthew's gospel.

### ❧ ISRAEL AT THE TIME OF SAMUEL ❧

*This book covers the life of Samuel, the last of the Judges and first of the prophets, and the lives of the Israelite kings he anointed.*

THE EARLY LIFE OF SAMUEL
*First Book of Samuel, Ch. 1 to 7.*
KING SAUL
*First Book of Samuel, Ch. 8 to 15.*
SAUL AND DAVID
*First Book of Samuel, Ch. 16 to 31.*
BATTLE FOR THE CROWN
*Second Book of Samuel, Ch. 2 to 4.*
KING DAVID
*Second Book of Samuel, Ch. 4 to 20.*
KING SOLOMON
*First Book of Kings, Ch. 1 to 11.*
THE KINGDOM IS DIVIDED
*First Book of Kings, Ch. 12.*

**David and Jonathan**
The fugitive David was the closest of friends with Jonathan, even though Jonathan was the son of King Saul, who wanted to kill him.

**Judea and the Dead Sea**
The Salt Sea, now called the Dead Sea, and the River Jordan are at the centre of the Promised Land, and have been important since the miraculous crossing of the river by Joshua. The shores of the Salt Sea are actually 400m below sea level.

# Israel in the Time of Samuel

THERE were great changes to the state of Israel during the life of Samuel. When he was first called by God, the Israelites had long since fallen into sinful habits. They were worshipping other gods, the same gods that the Lord told them never to worship when they first arrived in Canaan under the leadership of Joshua.

When Samuel became the last Judge of Israel, the Israelites were fighting a losing battle with the Philistines, one of the tribes already living in Canaan. The Philistines were one of the first people to use iron in their weapons. They had a better organized army and were winning land from the Israelites. This stopped when Samuel took command. His first battle with the Philistines, with help from God and the Israelites with their renewed faith, was a huge success. For the rest of Samuel's life the Philistines were forced further and further east towards the sea.

All the lands around Israel at this time were kingdoms, and most were successful in battle, much of the time against the Israelites. Many of the people thought that this was because the Israelites did not have a single, strong leader to stand at the head of their army. They asked Samuel for a king, and he anointed Saul.

Saul won his first victory against the Ammonites who were laying siege to the city of Jabesh-gilead. This was the first of many victories for Saul, who won many cities for Israel. He won a great victory in the battle at Michmash, when his son Jonathan led the outnumbered Israelites against the powerful Philistine army. Saul also met with success in the south of the kingdom, winning battles with other tribes like the Edomites and the Moabites.

Despite his military successes for the Israelites, Saul was never as successful in leading the Israelites in their worship of God. Samuel was always the religious head of the country. This led to problems for Saul, who offended God and Samuel time after time. God eventually abandoned Saul as king, and blessed David instead. After Saul's death at Gilboa, and a brief civil war for the crown between David and Saul's surviving son, Rehoboam, David ruled the whole of Israel as the sole king.

David first made sure that the land Saul had gained from the surrounding tribes was safe, and went on to win more land, from the Philistines, the Edomites, the Ammonites, the Moabites, and the Arameans in the north. When he captured Jerusalem and made it his capital, the Israelites' conquest of Canaan was finally complete.

David did not stop there. He had extended the kingdom, but he also expanded the 'vassal territories' of Israel. These were states or kingdoms that paid sums of money to David so that he would not attack them, and David would also provide them with protection from other invading states. David extended the empire from Ezion-geber in the south, to Damascus in the north. At his death, he handed on to his son Solomon an empire larger than any that the Israelites would ever see again.

Solomon was not the man of war that his father had been. He secured the lands that his father had gained, and made peace treaties with the surrounding powers to ensure that his kingdom was safe. Solomon divided his kingdom into twelve districts, each with its own governors to collect taxes and organize the forced-labour schemes, where people had to leave their land and work for Solomon for one month in three. By getting the country organized like this, he could claim taxes from the people, which funded his building work. But the heavy taxes and forced labour made him unpopular.

When his son, Rehoboam came to the throne and told the people he would be even worse than his father, ten of the tribes rebelled and crowned Jeroboam, one of Solomon's governors, their king. This split Israel into two countries. The northern country kept the name of Israel, and built their capital city at Samaria. The southern country was made up of the two tribes of Benjamin and Judah. They took the name of Judah, with their capital at Jerusalem.

**The Promised Land**
The picture on the left is an old map of the Promised Land. It shows the Salt Sea, the River Jordan and the Sea of Chinnereth on the right-hand side. You can also see Egypt and the River Nile on the left.

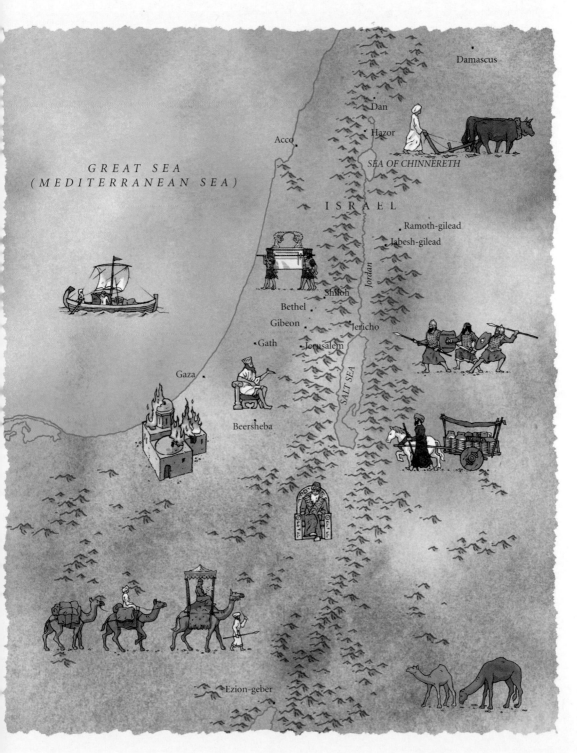

GREAT SEA
(MEDITERRANEAN SEA)

Damascus

Dan

Hazor

Acco

SEA OF CHINNERETH

I S R A E L

Ramoth-gilead

Jabesh-gilead

Jordan

Shiloh

Bethel

Gibeon

Jericho

Gath

Jerusalem

SALT SEA

Gaza

Beersheba

Ezion-geber

# The Birth of Samuel

AFTER the Israelites had settled into the Promised Land, they began to forget God. People ignored the warnings of the Judges. They sank into sinful habits, worshipping false idols. Eventually, few God-fearing families were left. Even old Eli – the high priest in the tabernacle at Shiloh – had two wicked sons. Hophni and Phinehas were priests themselves, but they had no respect for God. They were dishonest and violent, and even took the sacrifices worshippers brought for the Lord, beating up anyone who resisted.

Only a few people still kept the Lord's commands. Among them were Elkanah and his two wives, Peninnah, who had many children, and Hannah, who had none. Each year, the family would travel from their home in the hills to worship God in the tabernacle at Shiloh. And each year, Hannah would pray with all her heart that the Lord would grant her children. One year, after Peninnah had teased her about being childless, Hannah was more distressed than usual. She stood in the house of the Lord begging God to answer her. "Lord," she vowed, "if you'll grant me a son, I promise I'll give him into your service."

When Eli noticed her muttering under her breath, he was furious. He was always having to throw thugs out of the shrine, and now a drunk had wandered in. "Get out of God's house and don't come back till you've sobered up!" he yelled furiously at Hannah.

"Please forgive me, my lord, I'm not drunk," sobbed Hannah, and poured out her heart to the old priest.

"Go in peace," he said kindly, "and may you have your wish. I'll add my prayers to yours."

Imagine Hannah's joy soon after when she realized she was pregnant! She called the boy Samuel, and a couple of years later, she kept her promise to God. Hannah went back to Shiloh and gave the boy into Eli's hands. God rewarded Hannah's loyalty by sending her five other children, and each year she returned to Shiloh to see her firstborn son.

Samuel grew up pure-hearted and strong. He loved the old priest as if he were his real father, and Eli was as proud of Samuel as he was ashamed of his own sons. "Why do you commit these terrible crimes?"Eli raged at Hophni and Phinehas. But they just ignored the old man and carried on regardless.

One day a man arrived in Shiloh, asking for Eli. The days of great prophets such as Moses and Joshua were long gone. However, Eli knew the stranger was a prophet. The prophet's message made Eli's blood run cold.

"Centuries ago, God appointed your family as priests to serve Him for ever. Now your sons are sinning against

**Priests and worshippers**
As priests, Eli's sons were entitled to some of the sacrificial offerings brought to the tabernacle. They abused their position by taking more than their proper share, and because of their sinful acts, God put a curse on Eli's family.

Him. Know then that sickness, poverty and misery will soon arrive at your door. Both your sons will die on the same day, and the Lord will raise up a new, faithful priest who will serve Him truly."

From then on, Eli had a heavy heart. And as his spirit sank, he started to lose his sight, but Samuel was always close at hand to help the old man.

One night when Samuel was lying in bed he heard someone calling his name. Samuel ran to the high priest straight away. But the old man was puzzled.

"I didn't call you," Eli said. "Go and lie down again."

Samuel had just settled down when the voice came again. "Samuel! Samuel!" Once more, Samuel leapt up and raced round to Eli's room.

> ‘I will fulfil against Eli all that I have spoken concerning his house.’

"Here I am, father," he told the old man.

"I didn't call, my son," replied Eli. "Go back to sleep now." But when it happened a third time, a shiver ran down Eli's spine. He suddenly realized what was going on.

"Go and lie down," he told Samuel gently. "If someone calls you again, say, 'Speak, Lord, for your servant is listening.'"

When Samuel heard the voice again, he replied just as Eli had told him, and the Lord spoke clearly into his mind.

"I am about to punish Israel for their lack of faith. Also tell Eli I am about to punish his family, because of his sons' evil deeds, which he knew about but failed to stop."

Samuel was worried. How could he possibly give the old man such dreadful news? "You must tell me everything that the Lord said," Eli insisted. Sadly, he listened to everything that was going to happen. He sighed wearily. "It's the Lord's will," murmured Eli. "He must do whatever He sees fit."

**Sacrificial fork**
This sacrificial fork would have been used by the priests to scoop up the parts of the sacrifice to which they were entitled.

**Hannah's song**
When Hannah took Samuel to Shiloh and gave him into God's service, she sang a song of praise and thanksgiving to the Lord. The words of the song suggest that she was a prophetess. Hannah's song has been compared to the song of thanksgiving that Mary sang when an angel told her she would become the mother of Jesus.

### ∼THE SONG OF HANNAH∼

THE LORD MAKES POOR
AND MAKES RICH;
HE BRINGS LOW, HE ALSO EXALTS.
HE RAISES UP THE POOR
FROM THE DUST;
HE LIFTS THE NEEDY
FROM THE ASH HEAP,
TO MAKE THEM SIT WITH PRINCES
AND INHERIT
A SEAT OF HONOUR.
FOR THE PILLARS OF THE EARTH
ARE THE LORD'S,
AND ON THEM HE HAS SET
THE WORLD. ∼

**Home of the tabernacle**
This is Shiloh, where the tabernacle was kept, and where Hannah went to pray. Its modern name is Seilun. The tabernacle was set up here by Joshua when the Israelites conquered Canaan and did not move until the time of King David.

# Philistines Capture the Ark

As Samuel grew up, he became known far and wide as a true prophet. Eli the high priest was getting frail and blind. His one hope was that Samuel would prove to be God's chosen new leader. Everything else looked gloomy.

The Philistines wanted to win back their land and were about to attack once again. The Israelite army was going to meet them, confident that God would be with them and give them victory. However, despite Samuel's rousing preaching, many people still worshipped idols. In the past, whenever the Israelites had turned away from God, God had turned His back on them too. Now, He left them to face their worst enemy alone.

At the end of the first battle 4,000 Israelite soldiers lay dead at the feet of the cheering Philistines. The elders were shocked. "Why did God allow us to be crushed like this?"

they groaned. "We'll have to bring the Ark of the Covenant here. We must have God with us on the battlefield if we are to be saved from our enemies."

The two wicked sons of Eli brought the holy ark from Shiloh. As the ark entered the camp, the soldiers cheered so loudly that the Philistines heard it in their own base. When they found out the cause of the commotion, they shook in their shoes. "The Israelite God who struck down the mighty Egyptians has come to help them!" they howled. "We're doomed!" However, instead of waiting in despair, they looked death straight in the eye. "Fight, Philistines!" came the command from their generals. "Don't be taken like slaves, but die with honour!" The soldiers launched a sudden, courageous attack.

Later that day, Eli was sitting worrying about the ark. "I should never have let them take it," he murmured. Then, he heard wailing, and footsteps hurrying towards him. "I come from the battlefield," the messenger panted.

Eli gripped his seat and tried to steady himself. "What's happened?" he asked.

"There's been a terrible slaughter!" the messenger wept. "30,000 foot soldiers have been slain and your sons are among them!"

Eli's heart was pounding. "What news of the ark?" he yelled, in a frenzy.

The messenger looked up at the high priest. "It has been

**Travels of the ark**
The ark was moved from Shiloh when the Israelites wrongly tried to use it as a good luck charm in battle. The Philistines captured the ark at Eben-ezer, but plagues infested each city it was kept in, so it was sent back to the Israelites at Beth-shemesh.

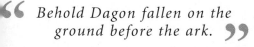

captured!" he whispered. Eli gasped and toppled backwards as if he'd been punched. There was a snap as the old man's neck cracked and Eli died, God's judgement on his family fulfilled.

The Philistines carried the ark to Ashdod, where their lords displayed it in the temple of their god, Dagon. However, next morning, the people found the statue of Dagon fallen face down on the floor before the ark. The Philistines set their god back in its place and dusted him off. The following day Dagon was again found lying in front of the ark, with his head and hands broken off. Soon ordinary people discovered lumps growing inside them and their skin breaking out in boils. Then thousands of rats scuttled into the city. "It's the ark!" the people wailed. "Get rid of it!"

> *Behold Dagon fallen on the ground before the ark.*

"They may be right," the lords agreed. "We'll send the ark to Gath instead."

The people of Gath fared no better. No sooner was the ark within their walls than the tumours and boils began to plague them too. "Take it away!" the inhabitants screamed.

The people of Ekron heard of plans to transfer the ark to them, and immediately they sent a committee to stop them. "Don't you dare send us that cursed thing!" they raged.

The Philistine lords sighed. "There's only one thing for it: we'll have to give it back to the Israelites."

The lords consulted magicians on how to return the ark. They built a cart to carry it, with an offering of ten golden statues. They hitched up two cows that they'd separated from their calves. "Set the cart off without a driver," the magicians instructed. "If the cows go to the border, it will prove the Israelite God really is in charge. If they return to their calves, we'll know it's all a load of rubbish."

The Philistines were stunned to see the cows plod straight down the road to the Israelite city of Beth-shemesh, just as if the cart had an invisible driver. The Israelites in the fields couldn't believe their eyes. Weeping with joy, they ran to receive their nation's treasure. And the ark stayed in a safe-house at nearby Gibeath-kiriath-jearim for 20 years, for the people dared not move it.

## Plagues
The offering of golden statues mentioned in the story included five gold rats, each one representing one of the five Philistine rulers. The Philistines hoped that by sending out statues of the rats that were carrying the plague, they would succeed in getting rid of the plague itself. The gold offerings were placed in the cart, in a box beside the ark.

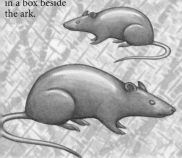

> SOME PEOPLE REFUSE TO HONOUR OR SERVE GOD. THE BIBLE TELLS US THAT EVENTUALLY EVERYONE WILL HAVE TO ADMIT THAT HE EXISTS AND IS WORTHY OF WORSHIP. ALL WILL BOW BEFORE HIM – AS THE STATUE OF DAGON DID.

## Ark in battle
The ark was the Israelites' most precious possession. By using the sacred ark as a talisman to protect them from the Philistines, the Israelites showed disrespect to God. Their punishment was to lose both the battle and the ark.

# Samuel in Command

SAMUEL grew up a strong man, full of faith in the Lord. He became the Judge, or leader of Israel, just as Eli had hoped. The great prophets of the past—Abraham, Moses, and Joshua—had all spoken to the nation and inspired the people, and Samuel was no exception. One of the very first things he did was to call a huge meeting at Mizpah. "There is only one God," he told the hundreds of thousands of people gathered there. "You have seen what dreadful things you bring upon yourselves when you abandon the Lord. Now, if you really want to turn back to God, you must get rid of all the pagan idols you've been worshiping. You must beg the Lord's forgiveness and feel truly sorry in your hearts. Make up your minds that you're going to serve the one true God. Do your very best to obey every single one of His commandments and laws. Then the Lord will save you all from the threat of the Philistines and raise the whole nation of Israel above all its enemies."

As the people listened, they looked up with awe at the young man who stood in front of them. Samuel's eyes shone as he spoke of God, his whole body was alive with passion. "It's true!" they shouted. "We've sinned against the Lord! Help us to find forgiveness!"

Filled with hope, Samuel gave great thanks to God. Then he instructed the nation that everyone was to begin a long fast right there and then as part of their penance, and Samuel led the crowd in prayer.

Meanwhile, news of the massive gathering was reaching the ears of the Philistine lords. "You'll never get another chance like this," the spies reported. "Nearly all of the Israelites have gathered together in one place, and they're mostly unarmed! To top it all, Samuel is there too!" Without a moment's delay, the Philistine lords mobilized their troops and marched on Mizpah.

Samuel was right in the middle of making a sacrifice when a terrified Israelite scout came dashing up to him with word that the full might of the Philistine army was drawing near. Panic rippled through the crowd like wildfire. The people began to jump up in terror, turning this way and that, not knowing which way to run. Samuel, however, calmly continued making his offering to God. He didn't flinch even when the Philistine soldiers suddenly appeared on the crests of the hills all around, endless dark figures against the sky.

> ❝ *The hand of the Lord was against the Philistines all the days of Samuel.* ❞

As the Israelites' screamed, the Philistines began to charge down the slopes toward them, spears aloft, swords glinting in the sun. At the very last minute, when the Philistines were close enough for the Israelites to see their faces, Samuel finished his sacrifice and looked up to heaven, praying for help. The wave of roaring troops suddenly disintegrated into a confused mob of bent figures, who stumbled around with their hands to their ears. The Israelite screams died away into a stunned silence. While they heard nothing but the beating of their

own hearts, the Philistines rolled on the earth in agony at the mind-splitting thunder that came from the skies.

Once the Israelites had recovered from the shock, they rushed on the soldiers with renewed confidence that the Lord was with them. And victory was theirs. It was a sign that God was willing to forgive the sinning nation.

For the rest of Samuel's life, the Israelites defeated the Philistines in every battle they fought. All the cities the

Philistines had won back were recaptured by Israel, too. The nation's other enemies sensibly stayed well away.

The Israelites looked up to Samuel as one of their greatest ever leaders; they respected him as someone very close to God. But Samuel didn't keep his distance from the people. Each year he toured around the country, going from place to place among them. And the prophet won back the Israelites' hearts for the Lord.

### Samuel
Not only was Samuel a Judge and a prophet, but his name is also given to the two books of *Samuel* in the *Old Testament*. When he was a baby, his mother dedicated him to God, and he was brought up by the high priest, Eli, at the temple at Shiloh. He was first called upon by God while still a child. His leadership was later challenged by those who wanted a king as leader instead of a Judge. After some resistance, Samuel anointed Saul as the first king of Israel. He later anointed David as the next king. Samuel died in a place called Ramah, north of Jerusalem, and was buried there.

### ❖ ABOUT THE STORY ❖
*Samuel gives us here the perfect example of the supreme faith in God that the Israelites have been lacking. Even as the Philistines bear down on the unarmed Israelites, Samuel knows that the Lord will protect them, so he puts the Lord first, completes his sacrifice, and God saves them.*

# Saul is Made King

IN his old age, Samuel made his two sons, Joel and Abijah, Judges over Israel. But like the sons of Eli, they were corrupt. They took bribes from the people, and ignored the way the rules should have been applied. Bad actions were frequently said to be right and good deeds to be wrong.

Eventually the elders of Israel visited Samuel at Ramah. "Samuel, you are a great man. But we know that you are too old to lead us now," they told him. "However, your sons are dishonest. We don't want Judges anymore, we want a king to govern us, like all the other nations."

When the elders had gone, Samuel wearily closed his eyes. "A king, Lord," he sighed. "You'd think that to have you for a king would be enough."

"The Israelites are rejecting me, just as they have before," God replied. "If the people want a king, they shall have one. But make sure they know what they're getting."

Samuel called a great assembly of the people. "Listen to the Lord's warning," he told the Israelites. "A king will force you to work as his servants. He will tax you and take a tenth of all your grain and wine, flocks, and workers. You will weep and wail at how your king rules over you, but the Lord will not answer your cries. For in having a king, you are pushing God aside."

"All the other nations have a king," the people protested. "Why shouldn't we?"

Samuel realized they weren't going to listen. Inside his head he heard the Lord's voice. "Give these Israelites what they want," God said.

Samuel shook his head. "Go home, all of you," he said quietly.

Months later, up in the hill country, a landowner called Kish told one of his sons, called Saul to track down some escaped donkeys. Saul searched for days without any luck until his servant told him that Samuel happened to be nearby. "He might help us," he said.

As the two men approached the city gates, they were surprised to see a stranger coming out to meet them. They were even more shocked when the old man said, "I am Samuel, who you are looking for. God told me yesterday that you would be coming. Your donkeys have been found, so stop worrying about them. In any case, a few donkeys are nothing compared to the whole of Israel." Saul was puzzled. Whatever did Samuel mean? He was even more puzzled when Samuel took Saul and his servant to be guests of honour at a great feast, and insisted they stay the night with him.

Next morning, the prophet anointed Saul with oil. "The Lord has declared that you are to be king of Israel," Samuel announced. "You will rule over all the people and

save them from their enemies. As a sign that this message comes from God, on your way out of the city two men will give you news about your donkeys. At the large oak tree at Tabor, three men will offer you bread. Finally, near the Philistine garrison at Gibeah, you'll meet a group of prophets singing hymns. Then I'll meet you at Mizpah."

Everything happened just as Samuel had predicted, but Saul was no longer amazed at these strange events. He had changed and had a new faith in the Lord.

Nevertheless, at the meeting the prophet called at Mizpah Saul was terrified. He'd never seen so many people in one place before. "Hear me, Israelites!" Samuel shouted to the crowd. "It is time to select your king." He told the people to draw lots, so everybody would know that nothing unfair had gone on. Although it seemed like chance, Samuel knew that God was in control. First, the Israelites drew lots for the tribe the king should come from – Benjamin was chosen. Next, the tribe drew lots – and the Matrite families were picked. Out of all the Matrite families, Kish's was chosen. And finally, from Kish's family, Saul's name was pulled out of the hat.

> '*We will have a king over us that may govern us and go out before us and fight our battles.*'

Saul was nowhere to be found! The excited Israelites searched the area for their new king. Finally someone spotted him hiding among a heap of bags, and he was pushed forward. "Here is the king God has chosen for you!" bellowed the prophet.

**The kingdom of Saul**
This map shows in orange the extent of Israel during the reign of King Saul. The Israelites had held on to a lot of Canaan, but they had never defeated the Philistines or the tribe of Moab.

**Horn of oil**
Samuel anointed Saul by rubbing a special holy oil onto him. This ceremony was a sign that Saul had been chosen by God. Samuel would have used olive oil mixed with spices, such as cinnamon and nutmeg. The oil would have been contained in a horn made of ivory and gold.

SOMETIMES PEOPLE DO THINGS WHICH THEY SHOULDN'T. THIS STORY REMINDS US THAT GOD ALLOWS US TO USE OUR FREE WILL TO MAKE MISTAKES. HE ALWAYS STAYS WITH US TO HELP WHEN THINGS GO WRONG AND WHEN WE ARE IN NEED.

**❖ ABOUT THE STORY ❖**
*God had intended the Israelites to be a model nation, showing others what it was like to trust God completely. But the Israelites found it hard to trust God when they couldn't see Him. They thought a king would be better, but forgot that kings are often selfish.*

# Saul's First Victory

NOT long after Saul became king, part of his new kingdom found itself in trouble. When the Israelites had first arrived in the Promised Land, they had conquered many territories belonging to the Ammonites. Ever since, the Ammonites had been intent on taking back their land, and sometimes they attacked Israel's borders. Now, under the command of Nahash, Ammonite warriors had

besieged the Israelite city of Jabesh-gilead. The out-numbered citizens tried to save themselves by making a treaty with the Ammonites. "If you allow us to surrender peacefully," the Israelite messengers pleaded with Nahash, "we promise to serve you as slaves."

But Nahash was ruthless. "We will allow you to live," he announced coldly, "on one condition: that we put out the right eye of every Israelite in the city."

The inhabitants of Jabesh-gilead were devastated, and the elders begged for seven days to think about it. What a terrible choice they had to make: either face starvation and eventual slaughter by the Ammonites; or suffer torture, endure life in bondage, and bring utter shame on the whole nation. Messengers raced out of the city towards Gibeah and King Saul, knowing that the lives of their families and friends depended on their getting through.

When the panic-stricken riders burst into King Saul's palace, he wasn't at home. Even though Saul was king, he still worked as a farmer and he was busy in the fields. That evening, as Saul returned from his ploughing, he heard weeping and wailing in his courtroom.

> ❝ The Spirit of God came mightily upon Saul and his anger was greatly kindled. ❞

Hearing the news from Jabesh-gilead, Saul's anger rose with the outrage of God Himself at the brutal Ammonite threat. With his own hands, he slaughtered two oxen and hacked them into pieces. Then he sent them to every tribe

**Saul's victory**
Saul's palace was at Gibeah, but the first time his people needed him to lead them in battle was against the cruel Ammonites at the city of Jabesh-gilead. Saul mustered troops and made his way north through Shiloh, Tirzah and Bezek, gathering men. By the time the army reached Jabesh-gilead, Saul had a huge army and easily defeated the enemy forces.

**Working the land**
At this time, farmers like Saul would have used wooden ploughs. Poorer farmers had no metal, but wealthier ones had ploughs with iron blades. As a pair of animals (usually oxen) pulled the plough along, the blades turned the soil over and cut furrows in it so that seeds could be planted there. A light plough was an advantage as the fields were often stony. It was useful to be able to lift the plough over boulders. Large stones were used instead of fencing to mark the boundaries of a field.

Meanwhile, Saul split his forces into three battalions. Early next morning they attacked the Ammonite camp and took the tribespeople completely unawares. Just as the king had promised, by midday the fighting was finished. The ground was littered with the lifeless bodies of the Ammonites, and the people of Jabesh-gilead wept with relief at their narrow escape.

How the Israelites rejoiced! They had hoped for a king who would put their enemies to rout. Saul was the answer to their prayers. "Where are those unfaithful few who refused to pay our king tribute?" the people began to shout. "They should die for their lack of loyalty!"

"Calm down!" cried Saul. "You're not going to lay hands on anyone. This day is a day of celebration, for the Lord has saved Israel once again." The soldiers marched triumphantly back to Gibeah, with their glorious king at their head. They sacrificed peace offerings to the Lord and carried on the celebrations.

in Israel with the message: "Anyone who doesn't follow me into battle will find the same thing happens to his herds."

Israelites across the country felt the Lord was calling them to defend the land. Every fit man came out to fight. When Saul mustered his army at Bezek, he had 300,000 Israelite troops to face the 30,000 Ammonite soldiers.

Within the city, the terror among the people was growing quickly. "Don't be afraid," came the reassuring message from their new king. "By midday tomorrow, I promise you that it will all be over."

The people of Jabesh sent an envoy to tell Nahash that they would surrender the next day at noon. At best, the message would trick the Ammonites into a false sense of security. At worst, they would have to give themselves up and face the appalling consequences.

**Defending a town**
Towns in ancient times had to be carefully defended because of constant battles over land. Most towns were surrounded by walls which were 3 m wide and 6–9 m high. The walls prevented enemies from entering and formed a platform from which to attack. The picture shows a battering ram being used against the walls of a besieged city.

---

**❖ ABOUT THE STORY ❖**

*This victory helped the Israelites to see that they could rely on God to rescue them from their enemies. It also reminded them that He did not want them to become slaves again, as they had been in Egypt. Unfortunately, although this victory was entirely due to God's help, Saul began to think he had special powers too – and this pride led to his later downfall.*

---

# Saul and Jonathan

SAUL'S son Jonathan inherited his father's fighting spirit, and his battalion of 1,000 soldiers took the Philistine garrison at Geba. The nation's hopes soared. They could recapture more of the land taken by the Philistines! All Israel followed Jonathan's example and rallied to their king. But the Philistines sent for reinforcements, and soon 30,000 chariots and 6,000 cavalry had amassed at Michmash, vastly outnumbering Saul's army. Many of the Israelite volunteers lost their nerve and hid in the hills.

Saul didn't move until the prophet Samuel arrived to offer sacrifice to the Lord. After waiting a whole week, Saul decided to delay no longer. Even though only priests were allowed to offer sacrifices, he'd have to do it himself.

Just as he finished, Samuel arrived. "You have done a very foolish thing," the angry prophet told Saul. "Because you have gone against the Lord's commandments, He will take the kingdom away from you and your sons. Instead, a new king will be crowned." Then Samuel left the camp.

Things were bad. Only 600 Israelite soldiers remained, and only Saul and Jonathan had proper weapons – everyone else had axes and scythes from their farms. The Philistines were in no hurry to attack; they knew they could crush the Israelites at any time.

Jonathan could not bear the waiting any longer. "Let's go over to the Philistine garrison and see what happens," he urged his armour-bearer one day. Trusting the Lord, Jonathan decided that if the Philistines challenged them to come up to the camp, it would be a sign that God was with him, would defeat the Philistines.

The Philistine look-outs laughed when they saw the two Israelites approaching. They were sure they had nothing to fear. "Come here!" they mocked, drawing their swords. "We've got something to show you!"

Jonathan felt a surge of confidence. "God is with us!" he whispered. The two men attacked and soon 20 Philistine soldiers lay dead. They turned and began to make for the main Philistine camp.

At the sudden sight of the two Israelites, the Philistines were thrown into utter confusion. It seemed as if the enemy had appeared out of nowhere. The Philistines ran to and fro in panic, and in the chaos they ended up fighting each other.

## ❧ ABOUT THE STORY ❧

*When Saul became king, Samuel explained that God was still in charge; Saul was simply His servant. Therefore, the human king had to obey God's laws. To show that he did, the king was not allowed to offer sacrifices – that was the job of priests. Saul, however, decided that he could do what he liked. He tried to take God's place, and as a result lost the right to be king.*

SCYTHE    ADZE    CHOPPER    SICKLE

**Israelite weapons**
These are some of the tools the Israelites might have used as weapons. A scythe was normally used for cutting the crops at harvest time. An adze was a tool with a wooden shaft and a metal blade used for planing large pieces of wood to a smooth finish. An axe was used mainly for cutting down trees and chopping wood roughly into shape. The sickle here was also used to cut crops. It is made of wood with flint teeth.

Next day, King Saul went with a priest to ask God for guidance. Saul's prayers were met by silence. "Someone has sinned and so the Lord has closed His ears to us," the king announced. "Whoever it is will die." Imagine Saul's horror when he found out that it was Jonathan who had disobeyed him. The army yelled, "We don't want Jonathan to die for his mistake! Our victory over the Philistines is all due to him." The whole army fell on their knees, praying to God and offering all they had as a ransom for Jonathan. The king's son was spared, and the soldiers carried him home in triumph.

> ❝ *'Cursed be the man who eats food until it is evening and I am avenged on my enemies.'* ❞

Back in the Israelite camp Saul noticed the commotion and sent his troops on the attack. When the Philistines saw Saul's soldiers coming, they ran for their lives. "No one is to stop for food until every Philistine is dead!" cried Saul. On and on went the battle until nightfall when, faint with hunger, Saul was forced to make camp. But Jonathan hadn't heard his father's command not to eat. When he found some honeycomb as they marched he ate it.

**Saul's disobedience**
Saul's arrogance in taking over the role of the prophet and offering a sacrifice cost Saul dearly – his sons would not inherit their father's throne. The picture above shows priests offering a sacrifice.

SAUL'S COMMAND NOT TO STOP FOR FOOD WAS FOOLISH. IT CAUSED PEOPLE TO SUFFER AND NEARLY COST JONATHAN'S LIFE. THE BIBLE TELLS US NOT TO SAY THINGS WE MIGHT LATER REGRET. IT IS IMPORTANT THAT WE ARE HONEST WITH OURSELVES AND OTHERS, BUT WE MUST BE AWARE OF OTHER PEOPLE'S FEELINGS AND RESPECT THEM. ❧

**Jonathan**
This story illustrates the courage of Jonathan as a warrior, but he is mainly remembered for his loyalty to his friend David, who succeeded Saul as king of Israel. Jonathan was the eldest son of King Saul, and his loyalty to David conflicted with his duty to his father, who wanted David dead. Although Jonathan made several attempts at peacemaking, he was forced to disobey Saul to protect David. Jonathan died with his father during a battle against the Philistines at Mount Gilboa.

# Saul the Warrior King

KING Saul went on to win victory after victory. But he and Samuel hadn't spoken since the day the king had offered his own sacrifices at Michmash. So Saul was surprised when the prophet Samuel arrived at the palace. Samuel had a message from God. "When Israel moved from Egypt to Canaan, the Amalekite people attacked us.

God now commands you to go and destroy them. Have no mercy. Don't even spare their cattle or possessions."

Saul marched 210,000 fighting men to a valley near Amalek. He attacked the city and killed the people.

However, the Amalekite king, Agag, begged Saul to spare him. Saul also had second thoughts about slaughtering the Amalekite sheep and cattle. He added them to his own flocks.

Even before the king returned, the Lord had told Samuel that

SAMUEL'S STATEMENT "TO OBEY GOD IS BETTER THAN TO SACRIFICE" IS OFTEN REPEATED IN THE BIBLE. IT MEANS THAT RELIGIOUS ACTS ALONE DON'T PLEASE GOD: WE MUST OBEY HIM IN OUR DAILY LIFE.

### Destruction of Amalek
This picture shows the destruction of Amalek. The Amalekites had been enemies of the Israelites since their years in the wilderness. God ordered Saul to destroy them as a punishment for their repeated attacks on His people. He also wanted to ensure that the Amalekites would no longer be a threat to Israel.

### Sparing the Kenites
The Kenites were a tribe who had once shown kindness to the Israelites by guiding them in the desert. Because of this, they were spared by Saul. The name "Kenite" means "smith". The region the Kenites inhabited was known to contain copper, shown above, so they are thought to have been coppersmiths.

Saul had defied God. At once Samuel set off to find Saul.

"I've done it!" Saul lied. "I did what the Lord wanted."

"Why then can I hear the noises of cattle?" said Samuel.

Saul piled lie upon lie. "We took the animals so we can sacrifice them to God." he said.

"Stop!" Samuel bellowed. "You've disobeyed the Lord's commands! Why did you take some things for yourself, when you knew it was wrong?"

Saul still wouldn't own up. "I *have* obeyed God," he insisted. "My mission was to crush the Amalekites. King Agag is in my control, and I've wiped out his city. We've left the best of the livestock to sacrifice to the Lord."

Samuel was furious. "You should know that to listen to God and obey Him is much more important than offering Him sacrifices! Rebellion and stubbornness are terrible sins. You have rejected the word of God, and He has rejected you as king."

At that Saul panicked. "I'm sorry. I have sinned," he confessed, falling on his knees before the wise old prophet. "I know I should have listened to the Lord, and not worried what the people thought. I beg you, please ask God to forgive me."

The prophet was stony-faced. "The Lord no longer sees you as the king of His people." Samuel turned to go and Saul tried to stop him. He caught the edge of the old man's robe and it ripped. "Just as you have ripped my robe," Samuel declared, "so today the Lord has torn the kingdom from you. He is going to give it to a better man."

Even though Saul was king, Samuel was still the Judge of all Israel. He called for a sword and killed Agag, king of the Amalekites, on the spot.

Samuel returned to his home and Saul went back to Gibeah. The prophet grieved for Saul, but he would have nothing further to do with him. God was sorry that He'd ever chosen Saul to be king of Israel.

> **And Samuel hewed Agag in pieces before the Lord in Gilgal.**

### God's rejection of Saul

Samuel ordered Saul to destroy all the Amalekites, including all their livestock– their cattle and sheep. Instead of killing the Amalekite king, Agag, Saul took him prisoner. He also kept the best of the animals for himself instead of destroying them. Because of this disobedience, Saul was rejected by God as king and Samuel never saw King Saul again. Samuel had predicted that if Israel had a king, troubles such as this would arise. However, instead of being pleased at his accurate forecast, he grieved for Saul. The picture shows God telling Samuel that He is rejecting Saul as king, while Saul looks on.

# The Choosing of David

THE time came when the Lord told Samuel to stop feeling sorry for Saul. "He is no longer king of Israel," God told the elderly prophet. "I want you to take some holy oil to Bethlehem. Visit Jesse, for I have chosen one of his sons to be Israel's new king."

Samuel was worried. "If Saul hears about this, he'll kill me," he told the Lord.

"Pretend that you are in Bethlehem to make an important sacrifice," the Lord suggested. "Invite Jesse to the ceremony and then I will show you what to do."

When the elders of Bethlehem heard that the great prophet was coming, they hurried to meet him, wondering why he had come. "Welcome," they greeted Samuel. "We hope there's nothing wrong." Everyone feared the awe-inspiring man of God.

"Of course there's nothing wrong," Samuel assured them. "I'm here to hold a special prayer service and offering, and you're all invited."

The leaders of Bethlehem must have been surprised to see that the prophet invited Jesse's household, a mere family of farmers to the important service. However, they must have been even more jealous when, after the prayers and the singing and the sacrifice were all done, Samuel drew Jesse and his family to one side for a quiet word. "I'd like to meet your family," the prophet said. The embarrassed farmer felt very honoured, and introduced his sons one at a time.

First was Eliab. As soon as Samuel laid his eyes on Jesse's broad-shouldered, good-looking eldest son, he thought to himself, "Surely this is the new king of Israel." But God immediately spoke clearly into his mind.

"Don't be deceived by how handsome or tall these young men are. Remember Saul – he looks like a hero, but he's not a true king. I see people differently from the way you see each other. I value someone not on their outward appearance, but on their inner worth. I look at human hearts and judge people on what they're like inside."

Next, Abinadab came forward. The prophet studied his face. "No, not this one," he thought.

Then Jesse called Shammah. Again Samuel thought, "No, not him either."

Four more of Jesse's sons passed under the all-seeing eyes of God's faithful servant, but Samuel knew that none of them was the right man. "There must be someone else," thought Samuel to himself, and said out loud to Jesse: "Are those all your sons?"

"There's one more," the puzzled farmer stuttered. "My youngest, David. But he's out looking after the sheep."

"Go and fetch him," Samuel urged gently.

When David arrived, the prophet at once heard the voice of the Lord saying, "Get up and bless him, for this is the one." So, to the complete shock of Jesse and his family, Samuel drew out his precious ceremonial horn filled with holy oil and anointed Jesse's youngest son David as the future king of Israel.

> **The Spirit of the Lord departed from Saul, and an evil spirit tormented him.**

After the prophet had gone, Jesse's family remained puzzled by what had happened. However, no one could deny that David seemed different, wiser, and sure of himself, with a strange fearlessness.

At the same time that David was filled with God's grace, the Spirit of the Lord left King Saul. Instead, an evil demon came to drive him mad with worries, doubts and fears, and thrust him into deep, black depressions.

Saul's servants suggested a companion to lift his spirits. "David, the son of Jesse of Bethlehem, can play the harp quite brilliantly. He's also a brave young man – a good fighter. And above all, people say that he's close to God."

Saul sent for Jesse's youngest son to come to the palace, never dreaming that the boy would one day replace him on the throne. David seemed to be the only person who could relieve the king of any of his depression, and Saul grew to love him dearly. He made David his honoured armour-bearer and kept him close by his side. Whenever Saul felt gloomy, David would play the harp and bring some moments of peace to the troubled king.

### Anointing

This picture shows Samuel anointing David as king by rubbing holy oil on to him. In the Old Testament, a person was anointed to show that they were in some way holy or special to God. Objects such as pillars, shields and the tabernacle, could be anointed too. It was a sin to use anointing oil for any other purpose. Anointing was an act of God and, because of this, was a solemn and important event. In the New Testament, Jesus anointed sick people as a way of healing them.

### ❧ ABOUT THE STORY ❧

*The Bible implies that David did not know exactly why he was anointed. If it had been known, Saul would have tried to kill David, and others could have tried to capture the throne for David. The young shepherd still had much to learn before he was ready to be king.*

# David and Goliath

IT wasn't long before the Philistines waged war on Israel again. King Saul gathered the army together, and young men from all over the country hurried to the king's camp.

David returned to his former job of looking after Jesse's sheep while three of his older brothers enlisted with Saul. Jesse worried about them continually; his eyes always looked dull and tired. One day, David noticed his father packing some grain, bread and cheeses. "Take these things to your brothers, David," Jesse urged his youngest son. "Then hurry home and tell me how they're doing."

When David reached Saul's camp, he found the soldiers retreating in a panic, running from the battle line as fast as they could. David couldn't believe his eyes. He was nearly trampled underfoot as the last soldiers swarmed past him. Then he saw the enemy, and he understood. On the far side of the battlefield, standing alone, was the biggest man David had ever seen. He was nearly as tall as two men with colossal legs like tree trunks. He carried a spear the size of a battering ram, and his mighty body was clad in enormous bronze armour. "Who is that?" David gasped, rooted to the spot. The soldiers nearby explained.

"It's Goliath of Gath," they told David. "Each time we're ready to attack, he strides out and challenges us to settle things by a duel. He says that if any puny Israelite can beat him, then the Philistines will be our slaves. If he beats our champion, then the Philistines will take all of us into slavery. The king has offered a huge reward to anyone who'll fight him, including his daughter's hand in marriage. But who could beat such a giant?"

"I'd give anything for the chance!" shouted David defiantly, and he went to find the king.

At first, Saul was reluctant to let the young shepherd face the huge warrior. But there was something about the way David spoke that convinced the king he might not be sending the boy to his death after all. "God has given me the strength to fight lions and bears when I am looking after my father's sheep," David said, "and now I know He'll give me the strength to beat this giant!" So Saul gave David permission to go and try.

The king dressed the shepherd for the battle, but David wasn't very big and Saul's armour totally swamped him. David could hardly move. And the weight of Saul's hefty sword and shield made his arms ache. So David took off all the equipment again, until he stood there in his simple shepherd's robe, holding only his sling, his crook and a bag of five smooth, round stones.

When he saw the tiny figure coming out to meet him, Goliath threw back his head and laughed. "Am I a dog, that you come with a stick to beat me?" he roared. "Come on then," he taunted. "I'll mince you into little pieces and feed you to the wild beasts." David was completely unruffled by the huge soldier.

> ❝ *David prevailed over the Philistine with a sling and a stone and killed him.* ❞

"You may have mighty weapons, but I'm armed with the most mighty weapon of them all, the name of the

### ❖ ABOUT THE STORY ❖

*David's anger was because Goliath was mocking God, not just frightening the people. The Israelites had forgotten that God was more powerful than any enemy. David had known God's protection and help in the past and was convinced that God would not let him down. David's faith in the power of God meant that, armed only with a sling and stones, he could single-handedly do what the whole Israelite army could not.*

**Single combat**
The practice of single combat was sometimes used to decide who should win a war or battle. In single combat, each side chose an individual to represent them. The above picture shows two knights fighting this sort of duel, with the armies facing each other.

Lord God of Israel! It's you who will be fed to the birds and wild beasts, not me!"

At these cheeky words, Goliath gave a mighty roar and strode forwards. David reached into his bag for a stone, took aim and slung it. The little pebble hit right in the centre of the giant's forehead, and it sank into him. Without even realizing what had hit him, Goliath keeled over like a felled tree and crumpled into the dust. David took Goliath's own huge sword, ran up to the massive body and hacked off Goliath's head.

On the far side of the battlefield, a stunned silence descended over the Philistine army. Then the jubilant Israelites charged, and the Philistines ran for their lives, all the way back to their cities.

DAVID ACTED IN FAITH, TRUSTING GOD TO HELP HIM. THE BIBLE ENCOURAGES CHRISTIANS FACING TASKS WHICH THEY BELIEVE ARE IN LINE WITH GOD'S WILL TO TRUST HIM TO OVERCOME DIFFICULTIES.

**Slings and stones**
The sling was a weapon used by many armies. It consisted of a wide pad with a string attached to each side. The soldier put a stone on the pad, held the ends of the strings in one hand and whirled the sling around very quickly. When he let go of one string, the stone flew through the air towards the enemy.

**Bears**
In the Bible, David tells Saul that he killed a bear and a lion that came to attack his sheep. For most of the year, wild bears eat plants. They only attack livestock during winter when they cannot find enough food on the ground.

# David in Danger

KILLING Goliath of Gath turned David into the Israelites' new hero. As the army marched home, the people of each city lined the roads, singing and dancing for joy. Everyone wanted to see the young shepherd who had killed a giant. The noise was almost deafening. "Da-vid! Da-vid! Da-vid!" the crowds chanted.

Saul had come to love David as though he were his own son, and Saul's son, Jonathan, was as fond of David as if he were his own brother. While the procession went on, Saul's old doubts began to niggle the king. The cries of

"We love you David!" were drowning the shouts of "God bless King Saul!" Saul became jealous. "If the people prefer David to me, it won't be long before they want him as king," he thought.

Next day, Saul sat slumped in a chair, snarling at anyone who approached him and muttering angrily under his breath. As usual David and his harp were sent for. David was gently plucking the harp strings when he felt a rush of air. A spear came flying at his head, and he ducked just in time. David tried to ignore the king's display of violence and continued to play as if nothing had happened. Then a second spear came hurtling at him. David again managed to dodge it, but he was deeply shocked.

The atmosphere in the palace grew worse. Since God had abandoned Saul, the king increasingly felt that his life was empty and meaningless. It was even more frustrating for him to see how David seemed to be always at peace, full of a quiet faith and courage. Eventually Saul could no longer bear to have the young man around him, and began to dream of killing David. Saul didn't want to stain his hands with the sin of murder, so Saul made David commander-in-chief of his troops, secretly hoping that he would be slain in a skirmish with the Philistines.

However, David never came to any harm. Wherever he went, he led his men to victory and his troops idolized him. All over the

---

### ❧ ABOUT THE STORY ❧

*The sad story of Saul's madness is told in the Bible to show two things. One is that when someone deliberately closes their heart to God, they open it to all sorts of evil forces. The other is that God looked after David in many ways. These narrow escapes show that God was protecting him so that one day he would be able to do the special job for which Samuel had anointed him.*

WHEN GOD CALLS SOMEONE TO SERVE HIM, HE ALLOWS NOTHING TO STOP THEM DOING THAT WORK. DIFFICULTIES DO NOT MEAN GOD HAS ABANDONED US. THEY MEAN THAT GOD CAN SHOW US HIS WORK. ↷

**A broken promise**
Saul had promised that whoever killed Goliath could marry his daughter. When David asked for his daughter's hand, Saul broke his promise and demanded an extra gift of 100 dead Philistines. He was sure David would be killed, but he returned unharmed and presented Saul with twice as many Philistine bodies.

country, Saul's subjects loved David more than ever before. The king just became more and more jealous.

One day, the scheming king was presented with the perfect plan to remove David for good. Saul discovered that David and his daughter, Michal, were in love. To David's utter astonishment the king said he'd like them to get married. After all, he was only a farmer's son. There was no way he could afford the traditional expensive present, especially for a king's daughter.

Saul grinned. "All I ask in payment for the bride is that you single-handedly slay 100 Philistines." The wicked king was sure that this time David would not survive. Once

> **Saul thought to make David fall by the hand of the Philistines**

again, David did the impossible. He killed not 100, but 200 Philistines. And Saul was forced to watch David marry his beloved daughter.

For Saul, this was the last straw. Now, above everything else, the king wanted David dead. He no longer cared how it was done or by whom. He was even ready to do it himself, never mind that it was a sin. Saul began to draw up a murderous plot with his courtiers.

Jonathan heard the palace rumours and raced to tell his best friend that his father wanted to kill him. He hid David away and then begged his father not to go ahead with his terrible plan. Although the king's icy heart

melted at first, it wasn't long before he was being driven mad with hatred again. Saul sent officers to arrest David and then, without a trial, to kill him.

Saul's daughter Michal was suspicious. She noticed strangers hanging around outside the house one night and immediately warned her husband. "My father's spies are everywhere. You must go," she wept. After a tearful farewell, David quietly climbed down a rope from the window and escaped into the night.

Next morning, when soldiers battered down the door, all they found in David's bed was a life-size statue wearing a goat-hair wig. David was far away, in the safe hands of God's faithful old servant, Samuel.

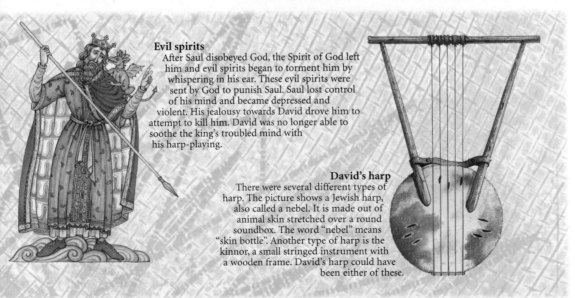

**Evil spirits**
After Saul disobeyed God, the Spirit of God left him and evil spirits began to torment him by whispering in his ear. These evil spirits were sent by God to punish Saul. Saul lost control of his mind and became depressed and violent. His jealousy towards David drove him to attempt to kill him. David was no longer able to soothe the king's troubled mind with his harp-playing.

**David's harp**
There were several different types of harp. The picture shows a Jewish harp, also called a nebel. It is made out of animal skin stretched over a round soundbox. The word "nebel" means "skin bottle". Another type of harp is the kinnor, a small stringed instrument with a wooden frame. David's harp could have been either of these.

# A Faithful Friend

SAMUEL sent David to a safe house at Naioth in Ramah. But Saul found out and sent soldiers after him. When they didn't return, the baffled king sent another group ... and then another ... Finally, wild with frustration, he set out after his son-in-law himself. But when Saul reached Naioth, he met the same strange fate as his soldiers. God's Spirit overcame him and he fell into a trance and took off his clothes. This allowed David to escape.

Apart from his wife, Michal, and the prophet, Samuel, there was only one other person David could trust to help him: the king's own son, Jonathan. He arranged a secret meeting with his best friend.

When the two men met safely, they hugged each other. "What have I done to make your father hate me so much?" David asked Jonathan.

Jonathan shook his head in dismay. "I still can't believe that my father wants you dead. If there's anything I can do to help, just say the word." David had an idea.

### ✤ ABOUT THE STORY ✤

*Many of the Bible's teachings are revealed in practical situations rather than given as a series of ideas. One of its chief teachings is that God is faithful to His people and that He expects us to be faithful to Him and to each other. In this story, Jonathan shows that faithfulness in a dramatic way. The story encourages us to trust God and to care for each other as Jonathan cared for David.*

**Bows and arrows**
Jonathan's bow would have been made of wood, together with animal horn and sinews. His arrows were probably made of reed, with metal tips. Arrows were carried in a leather holder called a quiver, which held about thirty arrows.

**Saul's trance**
When Saul arrived in Naioth, the Spirit of the Lord came over him and he went into a type of trance. God made him strip off his clothes because they were symbolic of his royal status, whereas in God's presence he was powerless. The Bible describes Saul's behaviour as "prophesying", which means revealing or interpreting God's will.

"It's simple!" he cried. "The new moon festival begins tomorrow and Saul will expect me at court. I'll stay here in the country. If your father asks where I am, say that I asked your permission to go and make a sacrifice with my family. If this doesn't bother him, I'll be reassured that I'm no longer in danger. However, if he's angry, then I'll know that I've spoiled some evil plan to get his hands on me."

"Yes!" cried Jonathan, eagerly. "I'll wait and see how he reacts, then I'll go out for my archery practice. Hide near the range. Once I've shot my arrows and my servant is collecting them, listen carefully to what I shout to him. If I yell, 'The arrows are near you,' it's a sign you have nothing to fear. But if I say, 'The arrows are further on,' then you're in danger and must get away fast." The two friends made a vow in the name of God that they would always remain loyal to each other, no matter what might happen.

Next day, at the feast, David's place at the king's table was empty. Saul didn't let it spoil his fun, but on the third day, when the king saw David's vacant chair, he exploded. "Where is David?" he demanded. Jonathan told his father the excuse David has asked him to give Saul.

David and Jonathan's plan didn't fool him. "You traitor!" he raged. "I know you're best friends! As long as he's alive, you'll never ascend to the throne that's rightfully yours!" Saul brandished a spear. "Bring David to me!"

Jonathan was seething. Stubbornly he replied, "Why should I? What has he done?"

The king roared and hurled his spear at his own son.

Next morning, full of sadness, Jonathan went out to the archery range. He shot his arrows past his servant, and as the lad searched for them, Jonathan called out, "The

 *'The Lord shall be between me and you for ever.'*

arrows are further on. Hurry up, don't hang about."

Jonathan sent the servant away, and David came out. Instead of greeting his friend with the usual embrace, David bowed low. It was the only way he could show Jonathan his gratitude for the great loyalty he had shown. The two friends knew it might be the last time they ever saw each other. "Go in peace," Jonathan said, "and may the Lord keep our friendship firm for ever." Then the two men turned away from each other and went their separate ways, Jonathan went back to his tyrant father at the palace, and David, the outcast, to life on the run.

---

### ❀ RELIGIOUS FEASTS ❀

*During religious feasts people gave thanks to God, repenting of their sins and offering sacrifices. These are the main feasts mentioned in the Old Testament:*

**The Feast of Weeks** *was later known as Pentecost. It was celebrated on the fiftieth day after the Sabbath that began the Passover. It was marked by the offering of sacrifices.*

**The Feast of Tabernacles,** *which was also called the Feast of Booths, lasted for seven days. It commemorates 40 years in the desert at the time of Moses. Fruit was gathered and people lived in booths, or tents, made of branches.*

**The Day of Blowing of Trumpets** *begins the new year. Sacrifices were offered and work stopped.*

**The Day of Atonement** *is when the high priest makes sacrifices to God to make up for peoples' sins. It took place on the tenth day of the seventh month.*

**The Feast of Purim** *commemorates the events of the book of Esther, when Queen Esther saved the Jews from a plot by the prime minister to kill all the Jews.*

# David the Outlaw

WHEN David left Saul for good, he disguised himself as an ordinary Israelite and fled to Nob. The head priest Ahimelech recognized him instantly and was suspicious. David pretended he had come without all the pomp of the royal household on the king's business. Ahimelech believed him.

Unfortunately, David saw in Nob, another of Saul's officers called Doeg. David knew Doeg recognised him, and David was unarmed. "The king sent me off in such a hurry that there wasn't time to gather my equipment," David pretended to Ahimelech. The only weapon the priest possessed was Goliath's sword. It was the sharpest and most deadly David had ever seen. David was pleased as he himself had won the sword from Goliath in battle.

It wasn't safe to stay in Nob, so David decided to hide among Saul's enemies. He fled to King Achish, the Philistine king of Gath, but his fame had gone before him. "Isn't this Israel's champion?" Achish's servants murmured, hauling David before the throne. He was among his enemies, and in grave danger, so he pretended he was mad. Luckily Achish believed David was mad, and threw him out of the court.

David was so famous that no matter how he disguised himself, he risked being recognized. He tried to avoid people altogether by going to the wilderness around Adullam. But first his brothers hurried to him, and then runaways sought him out. Eventually, David found himself leading about 400 men, many on the run, just like David.

Saul was furious that David was still free. One day he commanded everyone to assemble before him.

The king strode up and down the ranks, his face as black as thunder. "You are all so loyal to David that not one of you will tell me where he is?" he accused his men, in a cold rage. Doeg seized his chance to gain favour.

"I saw David at Nob," he told Saul. "Ahimelech gave him some food, and Goliath's sword." Saul's face lit up.

"You will be well rewarded," the king promised the smug Doeg. "Go and kill Ahimelech and his priests, then slaughter everyone else in the treacherous city," he commanded, "or die yourself."

Only one citizen in Nob managed to escape Doeg and his murdering troops, that was Abiathar, Ahimelech's own son. He brought the outlaws news of the terrible massacre. David wanted revenge at once, but the Israelite city of Keilah was besieged by the Philistines and God asked

## ❧ ABOUT THE STORY ❧

*This story shows the readers the contrast between Saul and David. Saul, appointed by God as king, is behaving selfishly. David, who was told by the prophet Samuel that he will be king one day, is willing to wait and refuses to take the law into his own hands. He will not kill Saul to make Samuel's promise come true, because he believes it is wrong to do so.*

### Cave shelter

The cave where David and his men hid, and where he cut off part of Saul's robe, was at a place called En-gedi, a fresh water spring west of the Salt Sea. The Hebrew word "en-gedi" means "spring of the kid" A "kid" here means a young goat. The place was home to wild goats, but the rugged ground and availability of water made it equally good as a hiding place for people. During excavations that took place in 1949 and 1961-5, several fortresses and a synagogue were discovered on the site.

The king broke down and wept. "You have repaid evil with kindness," he sobbed, "and you will truly be a great king one day. I ask you only to vow that you won't destroy my family for the evil that I have done to you." David gladly gave Saul the promise he wished for and the two men parted in peace, at least for the time being.

> **'The Lord gave you today into my hand in the cave, but I spared you.'**

David to rescue it. David's fighters saved hundreds of Israelites, even though they were risking their lives by leaving their hiding place in the hills.

Saul was overjoyed. "How stupid David is to walk into a walled and gated city," he laughed. Saul sent soldiers to Keilah, to capture David, but David and his band raced away. God had warned them of the king's approach.

Saul kept looking for David. As he was walking out of a dark cave he heard a familiar voice shout his name. Shocked, he spun round to see David at the cave-mouth, waving a piece of cloth. The outlaws had been hiding in the gloom, and David had crept up to the king and cut off a piece of Saul's robe without him knowing. David bowed down, as always. "Why do you listen to those who say I would hurt you?" he called out to Saul. "See, today I could have cut your throat, but I cut only your robe instead."

IT IS OFTEN TEMPTING TO GRAB IN A WRONG WAY SOMETHING WE BELIEVE SHOULD BE OURS. THE BIBLE TEACHES THAT WE CANNOT ACHIEVE GOOD ENDS BY USING BAD MEANS.

**David runs from Saul**
David escaped from Saul at Gibeah and was taken by Samuel to Ramah. He met his friend Jonathan at Horesh, before he fled to Nob. After seeking refuge with the Philistine king at Gath, David hid in the wilderness around Adullam, before he rescued the town of Keilah. He finally found Saul in the cave at En-gedi.

# David and Abigail

THE time came when the elderly prophet Samuel knew that death was near. Samuel was revered through the all Israel.Grief-stricken people gathered at Samuel's house in Ramah one last time to hear what he had to say.

"I have listened to all your complaints and answered your request for a king," the old man wearily told the crowds. "Now your king walks before you, leading you on, and I must stop here. Always remember that God was deeply offended by your demand for a king on earth. You must still strive to serve God as best you can, or He will sweep you aside as he would a pestering fly, both you and your ruler. As a sign that what I say is truly the word of God, the Lord will today send thunder and rain to destroy your wheat harvest."

Later that day, colossal black clouds blotted out the skies and towered over the land. Spears of lightning stabbed through the gloom, thunder rumbled like chariot wheels across the heavens and raindrops like arrows flattened the crops in the fields.

The people of Israel trembled. King Saul shuddered. Samuel, the prophet and last Judge of Israel passed away.

When David heard the news of his old friend's death, he was deeply saddened. He was also now in even more danger. With the great prophet gone, there was no one with any power to stop King Saul doing exactly what he wanted. Even though Saul had called off the hunt for his rival, David knew that the

demons which tormented the king wouldn't leave him alone for long. It was only a matter of time before they drove him mad with jealousy and fear once again, and then Saul would surely set out once more to find his rival and kill him.

David told his band of men to move camp. They set off, never staying too long in one place and living off their wits. Sometimes they would risk approaching a nearby village to ask for food and drink. At other times, they would simply plunder flocks of sheep and herds of cattle that were grazing out in the open, taking animals they thought their owners spare.

When the outlaws reached the pasturelands around Carmel, they encountered many shepherds, each with a massive flock, who all said that they worked for an important farmer called Nabal. David could have simply allowed his hungry outlaws to help themselves to a few of Nabal's sheep. After all, the farmer seemed to own thousands! He thought it would be better to strike a bargain with such a wealthy man, rather than make enemies by stealing from him. David sent ten men to the sheep-shearing at Carmel to find the landowner and politely put forward their requests.

Now Nabal was a thuggish type of man, puffed up with his own importance and used to throwing his weight around. When David's messengers were shown in by his servants, he hardly gave them a glance. "Who is this David? I don't know any 'son of Jesse'," he scoffed, pretending not to have heard of the great hero. "He's probably just another runaway servant. Do you really expect me to welcome a complete stranger and his band of criminals into my home and invite them to share my food? Now go away and don't come back!"

Nabal's servants were shocked. How could their master humiliate the great hero like this? David was putting out his hand in friendship, and Nabal was slapping it away. The servants knew that Saul's former army commander

wouldn't put up with their master's insults. Though they begged Nabal to change his mind the stubborn man wouldn't listen. The servants imagined how David and his men would be putting on their weapons and galloping towards them at that very moment. In desperation, one of Nabal's servants went to confide in their master's wife, Abigail.

Abigail was as good-natured and beautiful as her husband was arrogant and ugly. She knew that Nabal's rudeness would be the cause of all of their deaths, unless she went quickly to beg for mercy. Hurriedly, she loaded several donkeys with 200 loaves, five sheep, sacks of raisins, grain and fig cakes, and two wineskins. And without telling her husband, she set off down the mountain towards David's camp.

Abigail had not got very far when she saw a cloud of dust approaching. As David and his men drew into sight, she leapt down from her saddle and knelt before them, begging forgiveness for what her husband had done.

David was touched by the beautiful young woman's pleas. "Go in peace," he told her kindly. "I am glad that the Lord sent you to me this day."

Abigail raced home, full of relief that she'd saved her whole household from death, but cross that her husband had put them in such a desperate position in the first place. She was even more angry to find that Nabal was completely unconcerned; in fact, he had thrown a great feast. There he was, right in the middle of all the merry-making, and roaring drunk. Fuming with rage, Abigail pursed her lips and stormed off. Next morning, when Nabal was sobering up with a head-splitting hangover, she told her husband what she had done. Nabal was instantly filled with a cold fury. His face turned white, his eyes glazed over, his hands gripped the arms of his chair like icy claws, and his , spluttering mouth froze into silence. He was paralysed like stone, and he died ten days later.

> ❝ *Nabal's wife told him these things, and his heart died within him.* ❞

When David heard that Nabal had died, he simply nodded. "The Lord has repaid Nabal for his own evil-doings," he said. "Things have come to a just end." But he couldn't get thoughts of Nabal's wife out of his head. David had lost his wife, Michal, because when he had first gone on the run, the outraged King Saul had forced his daughter to marry another man. Now David was reminded of Michal by Abigail's loyalty and beauty. It wasn't long before the outlaw began to woo Nabal's widow, and soon Abigail became his wife.

WINESKIN    FIGS    BREAD

**Supplies for the outlaws**
This picture shows the food and drink that Abigail gave to David. To the left is a wineskin, above are figs, which were dried and made into cakes, and bread. David could have just stolen Nabal's sheep from the fields, but chose instead to befriend the shepherds and make an honest request. Abigail's quick action saved her husband's life temporarily, but he died later, punished by God for his wickedness.

> ⋇ **ABOUT THE STORY** ⋇
> *David had been forced by Saul to live on the edge of the law. He never wanted to steal from anyone unless there was no alternative. He offered many landowners protection from the Philistines in return for food and drink for him and his men.*

# The Witch of Endor

King Saul once more lapsed into an angry, black depression and once again he ordered his troops to find and kill his rival.

The king fared no better than before. Under cover of darkness, David and two of his men crept boldly into Saul's base, right up to Saul's very bedside. Neither Saul nor his soldiers stirred. His army commander Abner and royal bodyguard slept all around him. Once again, David chose not to slay Saul. Instead, he stole the spear and water jar from his bedside.

Next morning, David called across the valley. "Abner! Why weren't you watching over the king properly last night?" Both Saul and his general trembled at David's mercy and goodness in sparing Saul's life.

Back at their hideout, David told his followers, "Saul will hunt me down wherever I go within Israel. The only way for us to have any sort of freedom is if we go and live among our enemies, the Philistines." So David returned to King Achish of Gath, this time as the leader of a 600-strong band of soldiers. Achish had no reason to think that David was trying to trick him as they were both enemies of King Saul. The cunning king gave the outlaws land on the border of Gath and Israel. He hoped that David would stir up trouble by raiding Israelite settlements for supplies. David was also crafty. He attacked Philistine towns instead, and made sure that there were no survivors left alive to report the events. When Achish asked him who he had been attacking, he lied. The king trusted David completely. He thought David had begun to attack his own country and his people would never forgive him.

One day the Philistine leaders joined forces to attack Israel, and Achish asked David to ride with his army. David pretended that he was pleased. Achish rewarded him by appointing him his personal bodyguard.

Meanwhile, in the Israelite camp, Saul watched the arrival of the enemy forces with growing dread. His own army was hopelessly outnumbered, and his prayers were unanswered. He felt that God had abandoned him, and he could no longer ask Samuel for advice. He was desperate. According to God's law, Saul had banished everyone who practised magic, but now he sent his servants to seek out someone with magic powers. They found a clairvoyant at Endor who claimed she could talk with the dead. Saul disguised himself and hurried with two men to the medium's house. "I'll pay you well for a message from the spirit world," Saul told her. But the woman was wary.

"If the king hears that I have been practising witchcraft, I'll be put to death," she protested. Saul swore in God's name that no harm would come to her. Nervously the woman asked who he wanted to contact.

Swallowing hard, Saul whispered, "Bring up Samuel." The woman shivered at the name. All her instincts told her not to try, but Saul insisted. So the woman closed her eyes.

Suddenly she leapt up away from Saul in alarm. "You've tricked me!" she gasped. "You're the king himself!"

"Have no fear. Please tell me what you see," Saul begged.

Trembling all over, the woman shut her eyes once more. "I see an old man wrapped in a robe," she replied. "He wants to know why you've disturbed his rest." The king bowed down. Though he couldn't see Samuel, he knew it was the holy man.

> " *Samuel said, 'Why then do you ask me, since the Lord has become your enemy?'* "

"I face my biggest battle with the Philistines yet," Saul said to Samuel. "God no longer speaks to me through either prophets or dreams. So I've come for your advice."

Samuel's reply was grim. "Since the Lord has turned away from you, why do you come to me for help? The Lord has already told you He has taken the kingdom away from you and given it to David. Moreover, the Lord is about to give Israel into the hands of the Philistines. Tomorrow, you and your sons shall find yourselves here with me!"

Saul was shocked to the core. If Samuel was right, then nothing in heaven or earth could save him or his nation. Samuel had never been wrong before.

**Magic**
In the Bible, magic is defined as attempting to influence people and events by supernatural means. Black magic, such as witchcraft, tries to achieve evil results. White magic tries to undo curses and spells, and to use supernatural forces for the good of oneself and others. According to the Bible, all kinds of magic are wrong and must be overcome by the power of God. Magic is not compatible with a relationship with God and living a life that pleases him. This picture shows a breastplate that was worn by Egyptian magicians.

### ❖ ABOUT THE STORY ❖

*The Israelites had been forbidden by God to consult people who claimed to be able to influence the course of events through magic. They were to rely on God alone. Asking spirits questions was dangerous, as it could bring the Israelites into contact with evil forces.*

# The Death of Saul

THE Philistine and Israelite armies hurried to prepare for battle. Tension rose in both camps. The Philistine commanders boiled with rage when they saw David and his men riding with King Achish of Gath. "What are these Israelites doing here?" they demanded.

"I can vouch for him completely," Achish explained. "David is Saul's greatest enemy and has lived in my lands for years now." The Philistine chiefs weren't convinced.

"We don't trust him," they said determinedly. "For all you know, he might make it up with Saul and turn on us in the fighting. Send him away at once, where he can be no risk to us!"

The king of Gath couldn't change their minds so he told David that he was to have no part in the fighting. David was secretly relieved. He hadn't wanted to fight Saul.

Everything happened as Samuel had warned Saul through the witch of Endor. A Philistine victory was never in doubt. Their mighty army slew the Israelites in their hundreds. Among the dead and dying were three of Saul's four sons, including Jonathan, David's best friend. Saul himself had fallen under the showers of Philistine arrows, and was terribly injured. Saul's armour-bearer struggled to lift him up and help him limp away, but Saul was bleeding badly and in too much pain. "I'd rather die than be taken alive by the enemy," he groaned to his servant. "If you love me, help me to kill myself and escape being tortured by these ungodly savages." His armour-bearer broke down, unable to carry out the dreadful task. So Saul summoned the last dregs of his energy. Moaning with agony, he hauled himself to his feet and heaved up his sword. Then with one final effort, he fell forward on to the sword, gasping his last breath. Once Saul's armour-bearer was sure the king was dead, he killed himself too.

> " *Saul said to his armour-bearer, 'Draw your sword and thrust me through with it.'* "

As the news spread that their leader was dead, the exhausted Israelites turned and fled. The Philistines hacked off Saul's head and stripped his corpse of his armour, sending the trophies in triumph to the temple of their god, where they were put on display. Then they hung the dead king and his sons high on the town walls of Beth-shan.

Next morning, the royal bodies were gone. The brave people of Jabesh-gilead had made their way through enemy territory in the night to rescue the corpses, remembering how Saul had saved them many years ago from having their right eyes put out. The body of the first king of Israel was returned to his country and buried honourably among his grieving people.

David was devastated when he heard the news, yet he could see how God's hand was behind everything. The Lord had prevented David from having any part in the death of the king. Now he mourned Saul, who had both loved him and hated him at the same time, who had grown arrogant with power and turned away from God, and who had been driven mad in the knowledge that God

Endor
Shunem
Jezreel
VALLEY OF JEZREEL
ISRAELITE CAMP
Harod
Beth-shan
Mount Gilboa
Jordan

DAVID'S LAMENT FOR SAUL MAY SEEM ODD. BUT DAVID TRUSTED GOD AND DID NOT ALLOW HIMSELF TO BECOME BITTER. IT IS AN EXAMPLE OF HOW GOD WANTS PEOPLE TO TREAT EACH OTHER.≈

**The last days of Saul**
Saul, worried about what would happen in the battle with the Philistines, found a witch at Endor to talk to the dead prophet Samuel. Samuel said he could not win as God was against him. Saul went with his army to meet the Philistines in the Valley of Jezreel, where he died.

had abandoned him. And David grieved for Jonathan, the friend he loved even more than his own brothers, who had defied his father to stay loyal to David.

David remembered how the king had loved to hear him play the harp, the one thing that was able to bring him peace. He thought of the perfect tribute for Saul and his son. He would compose a beautiful song in their honour, telling all about the mountain battle.

The song began:
"Thy glory, O Israel, is slain upon thy high places!
How are the mighty fallen!"

When David sang his song, gently plucking at the strings of his harp as he had done so many years ago in the palace for the king, he wept with sorrow that Saul would never again hear him play. He wept for the loss of his closest friend, Jonathan, a loss to David himself and to all Israel.

### ～DAVID'S LAMENT～

SAUL AND JONATHAN, BELOVED
AND LOVELY!
IN LIFE AND IN DEATH THEY WERE
NOT DIVIDED;
THEY WERE SWIFTER THAN EAGLES,
THEY WERE STRONGER THAN LIONS.
JONATHAN LIES SLAIN UPON THY
HIGH PLACES.
I AM DISTRESSED FOR YOU, MY
BROTHER JONATHAN;
VERY PLEASANT HAVE YOU
BEEN TO ME;
YOUR LOVE TO
ME WAS WONDERFUL.

**Philistine figurine**
This figurine was found in the Philistine city of Ashdod, and it represents one of the Philistine goddesses, probably a fertility goddess that they believed made all things grow, such as their crops.

**David's lament**
The song David wrote for his two friends, Saul and Jonathan, has been described as one of the most beautiful pieces of poetry in the Bible. It expresses great sadness at the loss of the men both as national figures and as personal friends of David.

### ⚜ ABOUT THE STORY ⚜

*Once again, David had a lucky escape, reminding him that God was always protecting him. He could not get out of fighting with the Philistines without appearing disloyal and risking being killed by them as a traitor. God helped him and used the Philistines themselves to get David out of a tight spot. After this, few would question David's loyalty to Israel or his right to be king.*

# David Becomes King

WHEN Saul was dead, David prayed for guidance. He heard the Lord telling him to go back to Israel, to the south, and settle in Hebron. The people of Judah welcomed the hero with open arms, crowning David as their king.

The eleven other tribes in Israel did not accept David as their ruler. The general of Saul's army, Abner, with the backing of his troops, had set Saul's surviving son, Ishbosheth, on the throne to rule the rest of Israel.

King David ruled Judah and King Ishbosheth ruled the rest of Israel for several years. But everyone knew that Israel should be united with only one king.

One day the two armies fought, and David's soldiers won. Abner escaped, pursued by Asahel, brother of Joab, David's commander. Abner was forced to fight him and he stabbed Asahel with great regret.

After this there was full-scale civil war. Gradually support for David grew stronger. Ishbosheth was a weak ruler. He had never expected to be king as Saul had been grooming Jonathan for the throne. But power had gone to Ishbosheth's head. Eventually, Ishbosheth even confronted his most ardent supporter, Abner, because he had married one of Saul's concubines. Ishbosheth was trying to control everything. The general erupted. "After all I've done for you," he yelled, "you're rebuking me about a private affair!" Abner had only respected Ishbosheth because he was Saul's son; now he lost even that little regard. Abner did admire David as a servant of God and a great leader. "From now on, I'm going to support David," Abner bellowed.

"And God help me if I don't do everything I can to put him on the throne over all Israel." Ishbosheth stood trembling as Abner stalked off.

David threw a great feast to welcome Abner and Michal, his first wife, to the palace. Abner promised David that he would speak personally to the leaders of the 11 tribes and win their support for David. Abner set off immediately after the feast.

Soon afterwards David's commander, Joab arrived. He was appalled that the king had befriended the killer of his younger brother, Asahel. "David, Abner's deceiving you!" he cried. "He'll always remain true to the house of Saul." When David refused to listen, Joab sent a messenger to tell Abner to return. When the general arrived, Joab asked him

### The murder of Abner
Abner was Saul's nephew, so he supported Saul's son, Ishbosheth, in preference to David. However, after quarrelling with his master, Abner transferred his loyalty to David. David's army commander, Joab, was angry when he heard that David had welcomed Abner, because Abner had killed his brother, Asahel. Without David's knowledge, Joab murdered Abner. The picture shows a medieval altar detail of the scene, dating from 1181.

### Hebron
Hebron is situated 30km southwest of Jerusalem and is the highest town in Palestine. Many important figures in the Old Testament were buried there. So, apparently, were all the sons of Jacob, except for Joseph. Hebron was King David's capital for seven and a half years, until he moved to Jerusalem.

> **All the tribes of Israel came and said, 'You shall be prince over Israel.'**

for a private word. As Abner bent to Joab's ear, Joab stabbed him. "Now I am revenged for my brother's death!" Joab hissed.

David was furious. He cursed Joab and honoured Abner with fasting, and people tore their clothes in grief.

More tragedy followed. Two of Ishbosheth's captains had realised that without Abner Ishbosheth couldn't rule for long. They wanted to gain favour with David, so they crept into Ishbosheth's house and stabbed him. Then they ran to David and proudly told him of their crime. To their shock, David was horrified. "Ishbosheth had done nothing wrong," he groaned. "You have killed an innocent man in his own house. You will die for your wickedness." The traitors were executed.

David was now the sole contender for the throne. The elders gathered together and anointed him. At last, the king God had chosen ruled all Israel.

**Anointing oil**
The oil used for anointing would have been oil from olives (below), mixed with myrrh and spices such as cinnamon (right) and cassia (bottom right). The recipe was made from instructions given to the prophet Moses. Ordinary olive oil was used in cooking, in lamps and as a medicine, but it was a sin to use the special anointing oil for any other purpose.

---

**❖ ABOUT THE STORY ❖**

*Once again the writer wants to show how David lived according to God's laws. In ancient times, rulers often killed potential rivals, and took revenge on their enemies. Joab was like that, but David wasn't. He didn't want to force his way to power. He knew that human life is precious. He had killed people in war, but when he had the chance to "live and let live" in peace time he did.*

# Bringing the Ark to Jerusalem

KING David wanted to mark the beginning of a new era for the unified country. He thought it would be wrong to remain at Hebron or move to Saul's palace at Gibeah. He decided to make Jerusalem his new capital city.

The Jebusites who lived there were afraid of being thrown out of their homes so they barred the gates against him. David sent some of his soldiers up a large water pipe into the heart of the city, and soon the gates were open. The king's men streamed in, and from that day onwards Jerusalem was known as the City of David.

Once David's new palace had been built, he wanted to make a proper home for the ark in Jerusalem. The holy chest containing the Ten Commandments had been kept in a village near the border of Israel ever since the Philistines had returned it.

David declared that the day the priests moved the ark should be a public holiday, and the people of Israel poured into the streets. The people sang and played tambourines, flutes and cymbals as the ark rolled along on its ceremonial chariot. King David himself led the way.

Then disaster struck! The oxen pulling the chariot stumbled on the rocky road, and the man guiding the cart, called Uzzah, reached out to steady the precious ark. Only the priests were allowed to touch it. As soon as Uzzah touched the ark, he fell lifeless to the ground. The shocked Israelites fell silent, reminded of God's holy power. The festivities were over for that day.

Uzzah's death made even King David nervous, and for three months he left the ark in the care of Obed-edom the Gittite. When he tried again to move it, he held a prayer service and offered sacrifices before the procession set off. The people came out to celebrate with even more energy than before. They sang and danced in the greatest carnival they'd ever held. Even King David took turns dancing with them. Quite carried away, he stripped off his clothes and leapt for joy before the ark of the Lord.

> **" David danced before the Lord with all his might. "**

Not everyone was enjoying themselves. Since Michal had returned to be the king's wife, she'd grown jealous of the other wives David had taken in her absence. She felt superior because she was King Saul's daughter, and she thought it beneath her to go and mingle with the common people in the streets. As the ark entered Jerusalem she stayed in her room in the palace, looking down on the revelry with disdain. Imagine her horror when she saw her husband, the king, half-naked and singing and dancing with everyone else! Things were never the same between Michal and David again. For the king loved his subjects and his subjects loved him, and he thought it right that he should be among them to pay homage to the God who ruled over all.

David and the priests brought the ark to where the tabernacle had been set up, the richly embroidered tent in which it had rested since the time of Moses. The king offered more sacrifices and prayers, and blessed the people. Then he distributed a gift of bread, meat and raisins to every person to commemorate the occasion.

---

### ❖ ABOUT THE STORY ❖

*When Uzzah died, David was partly to blame. The ark should never have been put on a chariot. It was meant to be carried on poles, which the priests rested on their shoulders. That was how they carried it the second time. Uzzah's death showed the people that it was important to follow God's commands fully. David had thought he could improve on what God had said. He was wrong.*

**Surprise attack**
Because of Jerusalem's position on a high plateau surrounded by deep ravines, the Israelites had never before succeeded in capturing the city. The Jebusites felt safe but David took them by surprise by entering the city via a water shaft. The picture above shows the possible route taken by David and his men.

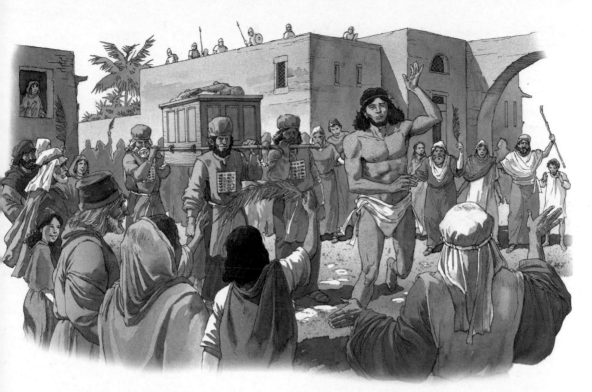

When David was quietly resting in his palace, he thought, "Beautiful as the tabernacle is, we need a permanent temple. My own house is made of cedar wood and covered in gold and silver. The tabernacle is only a tent." He shared his idea with Nathan, a prophet. The next day, Nathan told David that God had spoken to him in a dream. "The Lord says that the tabernacle will do for now. You are a man of war, and you should not build the holy temple. But one of your sons will be a man of peace, and he will build a temple to the Lord so glorious that people far and wide will hear of it." At this prophecy from Nathan, David was content.

**Death of Uzzah**
Uzzah made the mistake of touching the holy ark, which not even the Levites were allowed to handle. God was so angry with Uzzah that He punished him with death. The second time David tried to bring the ark into Jerusalem, he made sure that the Levites carried it according to the instructions that had been laid down by Moses.

**Jerusalem**
This view of modern Jerusalem shows the city walls, the old quarter, which is the oldest part of the city and the mosque called The Dome of the Rock.

# David and Bathsheba

KING David ruled justly and fairly. He won victories over his enemies, but was capable of great acts of mercy, too. Saul's son Jonathan had himself left a son, called Mephibosheth, who was crippled in both feet. David commanded that Mephibosheth and Ziba, the servant who looked after him, be brought to the palace. "I'm giving back to you all the lands that belonged to your grandfather, Saul," David told the amazed boy, kindly. "Ziba will look after it for you while you live here at the palace with me. For I loved your father as my brother, and so I will love you as my son."

Although David was a good and great king, he was still just a man, capable of sinning like everyone else. The day

finally came when David offended God, during a time when the Israelites were fighting a tribe called the Ammonites. The king had put the army in the capable hands of his commander Joab, while he stayed in Jerusalem to take care of things at home. David liked to stroll on the flat roof of his palace in the evening, looking out over the houses and hills of his beautiful capital city. Late one afternoon, he was pondering matters of state and admiring the view as usual when his thoughts were interrupted. Bathing in a pool in one of the gardens below was the most beautiful woman he had ever seen. For the whole evening afterwards, he found it impossible to concentrate. He couldn't rest until he knew who she was.

David discovered that the woman's name was Bathsheba and that she was married to Uriah, a soldier in his army, safely away at the war. David gave in to temptation and began to woo Bathsheba. For several months the two

### Amman – ancient Rabbah

Uriah and the rest of David's army were away fighting at Rabbah, the capital city of the Ammonites. Today, the city of Amman, the capital of Jordan, lies on the same site. The Ammonites had become a powerful people, but David and Joab succeeded in defeating the city and putting its inhabitants to forced labour. Later, after the death of Solomon, David's son, the Ammonites resurfaced as a threat to Israel. Today, many archaeological remains exist in and around Amman. Elsewhere in the city are ruins of cities from many different ages, including Roman and medieval. Among these ruins, sculptures and inscriptions from the 700s and 600s BC have been found. This picture shows a view across Amman from the citadel in the city. You can see the amphitheatre in the foreground.

### Perfume pot

After bathing, Bathsheba would have rubbed perfumed oil into her skin. Perfume was a luxury and was kept in special containers like this pot dating from the 900s to 800s BC.

lovers enjoyed a secret, romantic affair, until Bathsheba told David that she was expecting his baby. The king panicked. If Uriah found out, he would know that the baby was not his because he had been away. Everyone would soon know that David had sinned by sleeping with another man's wife.

The anxious king tried to disguise his sins. He sent a message to his commander Joab to send Uriah home, pretending that he wanted an update on the war. Uriah gave the king his report, and David sent him home. But next morning, the king found that the gallant officer had not slept at home with his wife. He had vowed not to return home while his men were still fighting, so he'd slept at the door of the palace.

Next day the king held a banquet for the soldier and plied him with alcohol. Surely if Uriah was drunk, he'd forget his resolution and go back to his wife? That way, Uriah would not know that the child was not his. But Uriah curled up on one of the king's couches instead.

David could not own up to his terrible sin. However, his next plan involved committing an even worse one. When Uriah went to rejoin his troops, David gave him a letter for Joab, the army commander. It said: "I command you to put Uriah in the frontline. When he is in the thick of the fighting, withdraw your troops so he is left alone among the enemy." Joab did just what David had ordered.

A messenger was soon on his way to tell Bathsheba that her husband had fallen in battle. And as soon as her period of mourning was over, David married her.

The king must have thought that he had got away with his crime, but God sees everything. The prophet Nathan came to see him. "Listen to this story," he told David. "Once upon a time a rich man owned lots of sheep, and a poor man had one little lamb, which was like a pet. One day, when a visitor came, the rich man took the poor man's lamb and roasted it for dinner."

David was angry. "He deserves to die for this. Who is he?" he cried.

> **6 6** *'Set Uriah in the forefront of the hardest fighting that he may be struck down, and die.'* **9 9**

"You," the prophet said. "And the Lord will punish you. You have sinned in private, but all Israel will see you suffer. In the future, your own children will rebel against you. But first, the baby will die." Sure enough, Bathsheba's baby was born weak. Though David prayed and fasted, begging God to save its life, a week later the infant died.

**O**NE REASON DAVID SINNED MAY HAVE BEEN BECAUSE HE WAS TIRED — HE SHOULD HAVE BEEN OUT WITH HIS ARMY. TEMPTATION IS OFTEN GREATEST WHEN OUR RESISTANCE IS LOW AND WE BECOME WEAK.

**Uriah's death**
David's sin in sleeping with Bathsheba led to the second sin of murder. If Uriah had gone to his wife, the child could have been passed off as his and David would not have killed him. David hoped once Uriah was dead, no one need know what had happened. But Nathan exposed the truth, and David was punished.

### ❖ ABOUT THE STORY ❖
*Until now, David has been shown as always loyal to God and anxious to do the right thing. In this case, though, it is Uriah who is right, and David who is very wrong. His lament over Saul could now be applied to himself: "How are the mighty fallen." The Bible never hides the failings of its greatest heroes. The stories are told to warn readers that everyone, even someone as great and as devoted to God as David, is vulnerable to sin.*

# Absalom the Rebel

NATHAN's prophecy that King David's children would rebel against him soon came true. David had many wives and children and was used to them all arguing among each other. But when his son Amnon attacked his daughter Tamar one day, it was serious. The family took sides and didn't forget the row. Two years later, another of David's sons, Absalom, took revenge for Tamar. He killed Amnon and fled to Egypt.

The king grieved for both his lost children. He couldn't bring back Amnon, but he could bring back Absalom. After five long years, David sent word to his son saying he was forgiven and that he could return safely to Israel, but on condition that he wasn't allowed to contact him at the palace.

For Absalom, this was worse than living in exile. He found it unbearable to think of all his brothers and sisters living as royal princes and princesses, while he lived in the same city as an outcast. Eventually, after three years had passed, David sent for Absalom. Absalom threw himself at the feet of the king, begging his father to receive him back into the family. David's heart melted, and he raised his son to his feet, hugging and kissing him. Absalom was disappointed not to feel the gladness he thought he'd feel. He remained full of a bitterness that wouldn't go away, and over time it grew and grew until it finally turned him against his father.

Secretly, Absalom decided to try to win the support of David's subjects for himself and overthrow his father. He was already a favourite with the people because he was a very handsome young man with long, thick hair. Each morning he presented himself at the city gate, standing on a horse-drawn chariot with fifty attendants around him. He would talk to the people and listen to their complaints, winning their hearts as a royal who did not mind shaking hands with ordinary people. "It's a shame the king doesn't come and chat to you all like this," Absalom would tell them. "He doesn't know about your problems like I do." And he'd heave a big sigh. "If only I were in charge, I'd fix things right away."

More and more people began to pledge their allegiance to the king's son, including those in the government such as David's trusted counsellor Ahithophel. Finally, even the bold Absalom thought that he was being a little too daring in organizing a rebellion right under the king's nose. He made an excuse to leave the city, telling his father that he wanted to go to the family city of Hebron to offer prayers and sacrifices for forgiveness. Then secretly he sent messengers to all the tribes telling his followers to come and gather there, for he was about to proclaim himself king.

However, many people still remained true to David, and word came to him of what his son was up to. He immediately fled out of danger by taking his court and leaving Jerusalem. Absalom moved in straightaway and set himself up on the throne. But what next? "Let me take some men and catch up with David," Ahithophel urged. "Your father will be unprepared and I can kill him without dragging anyone else into it. That way, you'll avoid civil war and your new subjects will be all the more pleased with you."

But a counsellor called Hushai gave quite the opposite advice. "No, you should bide your time," he told Absalom. "Your father is an experienced warrior and is probably hiding somewhere safe, away from his troops altogether. You have the throne now. Why not wait and gather a proper army around you? Then you can lead your men into battle and win all the glory for yourself."

Absalom liked the sound of that, and chose to follow Hushai. But unbeknown to him, the counsellor was one of David's men, working under cover to trick him with bad advice. And the king's son had fallen headfirst into the trap. Absalom's delay gave the king the breathing space he needed to rally his troops.

> ❝ The king cried with a loud voice, 'O my son Absalom.' ❞

Even after all his treacherous son had done to him, David couldn't find it within himself to stop loving his son. And on the day that the two armies finally clashed,

the king instructed his captains to take Absalom alive and not to harm him.

The battle took place in the thickly wooded forest near Shiloh, a dangerous place full of quicksands, poisonous snakes and wild animals that claimed almost as many lives as the fighting itself. When countryman had finished slaying countryman, and the victory was David's, over 20,000 men lay dead among the trees.

Absalom was not one of them. He had leapt on to a mule and tried to escape. It proved impossible to dodge the branches that barred the galloping animal's way. As the terrified mule turned this way and that in the dense undergrowth, Absalom's hair got caught in the trees. And when his mount finally found a direction in which to bolt, the king's son was left dangling from a branch while the animal shot away from under him.

Back at David's palace everyone was rejoicing, except for the king himself who was waiting anxiously at the gate for a messenger to bring news of his son. When he heard that his own army commander Joab had found Absalom and killed him, despite his orders, he broke down and wept uncontrollably. "My son, my son!" he wailed. "I wish that I had died instead of you." David was paying a terrible price for sinning with Bathsheba.

In the years ahead there was more trouble to come, God sent a famine and then a plague to make the job of establishing peace within the nation extra hard. There was some happiness, too. Bathsheba gave birth to another baby boy called Solomon, who comforted his mother and father a little for the children they had lost. David loved Bathsheba as his favourite wife, and Solomon was to become his most beloved son.

**Royal advisers**
Kings were often dependent on their advisers to help them make decisions. Absalom takes the wrong advice when he listens to Hushai.

THE BIBLE ENCOURAGES ITS READERS TO WAIT PATIENTLY FOR GOD TO GIVE US NEW OPPORTUNITIES, AND TO BE CONTENT WITH WHAT WE HAVE. IF WE TRY TO FORCE OUR WAY, MANY PEOPLE CAN GET HURT.

❖ **ABOUT THE STORY** ❖
*Absalom may have had his father's fighting spirit, but he had none of his patience and faith. Absalom became hungry for power and tried to force himself on to the throne. The writer wants us to notice that Absalom never asked what God wanted.*

# The Death of David

WHEN David was very old, he told everyone that he wanted Solomon to be king when he died. Another of David's sons had his own ideas. Adonijah wanted to be king and he talked several influential people into supporting him, including Joab, David's army commander, and Abiathar, the priest.

Adonijah thought that the old king no longer understood what was going on outside the palace walls, so he held a coronation ceremony for himself. Most of the royal officials of Judah attended the event. Nathan the prophet, who hadn't been invited, soon heard of it. He warned David's wife Bathsheba, and she went straight to David, who lay ill in bed. "You said our son

> **All the people said, 'Long live King Solomon.'**

Solomon would be your successor," she said, "yet Adonijah has made himself king. People are confused."

David took immediate action, which was quite the opposite to what Adonijah expected. Soon, Solomon was mounted on the king's own horse, wearing the king's crown, parading to Gihon with Nathan and Zadok the priest. There, they anointed Solomon as the new king, God's chosen successor to David. The appointment of the new ruler was proclaimed all over Israel.

People up and down the country celebrated. Adonijah heard the noise when he was in the middle of a party for his own coronation. As soon as his guests realised that the shouts of "Long live the king!" were for Solomon, they sneaked away. When David died and the rightful heir Solomon took the throne, no one dared argue with him.

## ✤ ABOUT THE STORY ✤

*Although the Israelites' request for a king had not been according to God's purpose, this story reminds readers that God did not abandon His people. He continued to guide them in the choice of the next king. The Bible teaches that God keeps His "covenant" or agreement with His people even when they are unfaithful to Him. God had a very special purpose for the new King Solomon.*

**Crowns**
Many different types of crown are described in the Bible. The crowns shown here are an Assyrian crown (left), above which are the red crown of Upper Egypt and the white crown of Lower Egypt. To the right is Ramses II's Egyptian double crown. Ramses had his own version of this crown made. In the top right corner is a simple Persian crown, and below this is a Syrian crown.

# The Wisdom of Solomon

SOLOMON was only young when he became king. But he was ready to rule. He knew how the civil wars and the strife with Israel's neighbours had taken their toll on the nation, and he wanted to keep Israel at peace. First he had his rival Adonijah and his supporters executed. Then he married the daughter of one of his major enemies, Pharaoh, ruler of Egypt.

Solomon trusted God, just as his father. One night, during a religious festival at Gibeon, God spoke to the young king in a dream. "What gift would you like me to give you?" the Lord asked. Solomon thought hard.

"Lord," he replied, "I wish to rule well. Therefore give me wisdom, so I can judge between right and wrong, and govern my people with fairness." The Lord was delighted with Solomon's answer.

 *The wisdom of God was in him.*

"Because you didn't ask for anything for yourself," God told him, "only for something that will benefit Israel, you will have your wish. I will also give you wealth, honour and long life."

One day, two women came to the king, begging him to settle an argument. They had both given birth, within three days of each other. But one night one of the babies had died. The first mother claimed that the other woman's child had died, and that she had swapped the dead baby for her live one while she slept.

"No I didn't!" the second mother yelled. "The living child is mine!"

"Enough!" bellowed Solomon. "Fetch me a sword." The two women waited. "The living baby will be cut into two and half given to each of you," he announced.

While the second woman nodded her agreement, the first woman fell on her knees before the king, weeping uncontrollably. "No, no, my lord! Do not kill the child," she wailed. "Please give it to her instead."

"Take your baby," Solomon smiled, laying the child in the first woman's arms. The king knew that the real mother would rather give up her child than allow it to be killed.

People were amazed by the king's good judgment, and he soon became known as "Solomon the Wise".

**Royal wedding**
Instead of marrying for love, Solomon used his marriage as a way of maintaining peace in Israel. He chose Pharaoh's daughter as his bride, as Pharaoh was unlikely to declare war on his son-in-law.

# Building the Temple

KING Solomon had new plans for almost everything, taxes, employment, the armed forces, trade, building. His greatest plan of all was for a great temple at Jerusalem, just as his father had wanted, a glorious home for the ark. It took four years just to lay the foundations of the temple. It was a similar design to the tabernacle, but twice as big. To complete the temple took another three years.

An enormous workforce was employed. King Solomon ordered many Israelites to leave their lands for one out of every three months to work for him. He also forced prisoners of war to become slaves. Soon thousands of men were cutting stone to size at the quarry. The great blocks were then heaved to the building site and hoisted into place so that not a single hammer or pickaxe was heard inside the holy building during its construction. For the really skilled work, Solomon hired expert joiners, carvers and metal workers from overseas.

Only the very best building materials were used. Rafts of the finest cedar and pine wood were floated down the coast from King Hiram of Tyre in Lebanon and taken inland by camel train. Merchants went to distant lands to trade Israel's foodstuffs and oil for gold and silver, rich fabrics and precious stones.

Eventually, all was finished. The temple was amazing. The walls and ceilings were made of elegant, sweet-smelling wood beams and planks. Rooms were lined with pure gold and carved with winged cherubim. Intricately carved doors of olive wood separated the sacred innermost chamber, the Holy of Holies from the outer room, the Holy Place, together with a shimmering veil that hung from delicate chains. The altar itself was made of gold.

Solomon dedicated the temple to the Lord with a grand ceremony. There were prayer services, and animals were sacrificed. The king prayed that God would make the temple a place that would inspire all who saw it to follow the Lord. He told the people that if ever they fell into the hands of enemies, they should look to the holy building, remembering what it stood for and who it served.

Finally there was a great procession as priests and elders of the tribes, with King Solomon at their head, brought the sacred ark of the covenant to its new resting place. As the priests laid it gently in the Holy of Holies, a cloud of God's glory filled the inner sanctuary. The Lord was present in the new house just as he had been in the tabernacle. The whole nation rejoiced.

> " *The glory of the Lord filled the house of the Lord.* "

When the celebrations were over, Solomon heard God say to him, "I have heard your prayers and requests and I have accepted this house you have built me. If you keep my commandments, I will establish your royal throne over Israel for ever, just as I promised your father, David. But if you turn aside from following me and worship other gods, then I will cause this temple to be destroyed and everyone will wonder how and why such a thing happened."

**Tools of the trade**
These pictures show an Egyptian stonemason's mallet (far right). Stonemasons cut and shaped blocks of stone. They used many of the same tools as carpenters, including saws, mallets, chisels and an adze, used like a modern plane (right).

**The temple's rooms**
The temple was divided into three areas: the entrance porch, the outer room (or Holy Place) and the inner room (or Holy of Holies). The outer room was a larger space, used by the priest for rituals and ceremonies. The inner room was smaller and was rarely used. Both rooms had wooden walls and doors, covered in decorative carving and overlaid with gold. Around the outside of the temple there were store rooms.

**Holy of Holies**
The Holy of Holies was the sacred inner room of Solomon's temple. This was where the ark of the covenant was kept. When the ark was taken into the Holy of Holies, the whole room filled with cloud, which signified that God was present.

Worship is not only a matter of going to a religious service or ceremony. We worship God whenever we do something just because we love Him and want to honour Him.

### ❖ ABOUT THE STORY ❖

*Solomon's temple must have been a beautiful place. The king did not build it to show off his skill and wealth, but because he wanted to give the best he had to God. The temple became a symbol both of God's presence among the people, and also of God's blessings to them. It was an act of worship in itself, because Solomon and the people sacrificed time and money to build it.*

# Wealth and Splendour

ONCE the glorious temple was finished, Solomon's building plans were far from over. He built a new palace with a massive hall where he could sit in judgement. With splendid royal living apartments as well, the palace was even bigger than the temple. The mountain quarries swarmed with labourers. Sparks flew from the desert blast furnaces, the roads groaned at the weight of materials going in and out of Jerusalem. The magnificent palace was made entirely of cedar wood and the finest marbles, with three tiers of windows to let the sun stream in and high ceilings held aloft by rows of pillars.

Then Solomon started work on a mighty wall to circle Jerusalem, thick and high enough to stand firm against foreign armies. He sent his surveyors to oversee the reconstruction of cities such as Gezer that had been destroyed in Israel's many wars. New strongholds sprang up from these blackened heaps of rubble. They were even greater than before, with thriving markets and public buildings. Solomon built new store cities to hold all of Israel's supplies and treasures. The Israelites filled new warehouses with sacks of grain, nuts and figs, which Israel's farmers paid as taxes to the king. They stacked cellars with barrels of wine and vats of oil, and heaped treasures and gems into locked safe-houses. Housing and training grounds were built for King Solomon's 1,400 gleaming chariots and 12,000 horsemen. On the Red Sea coast, Solomon built an entire fleet of merchant ships that travelled far and away to seek treasures, and returned with cargoes of apes, peacocks and ivory, rare woods and metals, and gleaming jewels.

As Solomon's subjects heard each new demand from their king, it seemed he was asking them to perform the

## ❀ TREASURES FROM ABROAD ❀

The Israelites traded with many other countries and brought back all kinds of exotic treasures, such as gold, silver, jewels and ivory.

**Bronze figure**
This is a Babylonian bronze statuette of a figure carrying a basket full of building materials. Figures like this were put in the foundations of temples.

**Stone lion's head**
This stone lion's head came from Assyria. It might originally have been attached to the handle of a fan.

**Silver goat**
This silver goat is thought to have come from Persepolis in Persia. It dates from the 400s BC.

impossible. They grumbled and groaned at the high taxes and the enforced labour. The king certainly wasn't loved by his people as David had been. Even so, everyone was impressed and overawed. The sailors and traders carried news of the king's greatness abroad, so that even people who weren't sure where Israel was heard rumours of its wealth, splendour and its greatest marvel of all – Solomon's wisdom. The king seemed to know all there was to know about anything. He could recite over 1,000 poems and quote over 3,000 proverbs. Statesmen and philosophers travelled to Solomon's court from far away, to listen to the king and ask his advice.

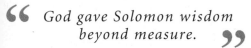

> ❝ *God gave Solomon wisdom beyond measure.* ❞

One of the visitors was the Queen of Sheba from Arabia. She had heard all the rumours about the king and wanted to know if they were true. So she came to see for herself, travelling with a great retinue of servants and carrying gifts of gold and jewels.

Solomon showed the queen everything, from his golden palace, throne and dishes; to how he ran his court with fairness and administered justice to the people. He showed her how the Israelites worshipped in their glorious new temple. He said he could answer any question she asked. The Queen of Sheba was left speechless. "Israel is lucky indeed to have such a magnificent king," she told Solomon. When she returned home, Solomon gave her many souvenirs from Israel's treasure houses.

**Solomon's kingdom**

During the rule of Solomon, Israel was more wealthy than it had ever been before. On this map the orange colour shows the lands of Israel. The dark brown colour shows the lands that paid tribute to Solomon. By this time, Ammon, Moab and even Philistia had all been conquered.

**Trading ship**

This picture shows a stone relief of a Phoenician trading ship. The Phoenicians were neighbours of the Israelites and, along with the Philistines, were leading powers at sea. The Israelites had little experience of the sea, so Solomon used Phoenician ships manned by Phoenician sailors to carry out his trading activities. The Israelites looked upon the ship as an object of wonder, and a safe journey was thought to be a demonstration of God's goodness and power.

❖ **ABOUT THE STORY** ❖

*Solomon had prayed for wisdom rather than riches, but God promised him riches as well as a special sign of His blessing. At this time, people assumed those who became wealthy were favoured by God. Later, they realized this is not always the case.*

# Fall of Solomon

ONE of the ways that all kings in ancient times showed how great they were was by having many wives. Just as Solomon outdid everyone in the splendour and scale of everything around him, he also outdid everyone in the number of women he married. Including Pharaoh's daughter, Solomon had 700 wives altogether. He also had 300 mistresses. It was not just because he was greedy. The king knew that all his plans for making Israel great rested on peace. The only way to keep the peace was to make treaties with his enemies abroad. And over the years, Israel had made many enemies. So Solomon kept his ministers of foreign affairs busy negotiating deals at meeting after meeting, while he himself married princess after princess. After all, it was unlikely that one country would attack another if the rulers were father- and son-in-law ...

There was only one problem. King Solomon's wives were from peoples such as the Moabites, the Ammonites, the

**Syrian storm-god**
Solomon had wives from many foreign lands, such as Moab, Edom and Syria. These women continued to worship their own gods, instead of the Israelite God. This is a stone relief of the Syrian storm-god, Hadad, standing on a bull and holding his symbol of a forked bolt of lightning.

**The Edomites**
This is an impression of the king of Edom's seal, from 800 BC. The Edomites were one of the tribes that attacked Solomon during his reign.

SOLOMON MAY HAVE JUST BEEN BEING TOLERANT OF THE OTHER RELIGIONS SO THAT HE COULD KEEP ORDER. BUT THE BIBLE TELLS US WE CANNOT BE TOLERANT OF ANYTHING THAT GOES AGAINST GOD. KEEPING THE TRUTH IS MORE IMPORTANT THAN KEEPING THE PEACE.

Edomites, the Sidonians and the Hittites. These were all nations with whom the Lord had forbidden the Israelites to mix. God had commanded this from the first days of the Israelites' arrival in the Promised Land. The foreign tribes worshipped pagan gods, and the Lord knew that if the Israelites intermarried with them, they would be tempted to follow the pagan ways.

King Solomon was no more able to resist this temptation than anyone else. As he grew older, he allowed his beautiful, loving wives to sway his judgement. He allowed them to perform their own pagan rituals and worship their own idols (burning holy incense and offering sacrifices as only the priests were allowed to do), and he even built special places in which to do it! First, there was a temple to Chemosh, the god of the Moabites. Then there was a temple to Molech, the god of the Ammonites, which Solomon had built on the mountain east of Jerusalem, within sight of the mighty Israelite temple itself! Soon pagan temples were being built all over the country, and every one of them with the full knowledge, and even with the approval of the king. Even worse, the wives persuaded Solomon to go and worship with them too. He didn't stop going to the temple of the Lord, but he was also often seen praying at the temple to Ashtoreth, goddess of the Sidonians, and Milcom of the Ammonites.

God was furious with him. How could the man on whom He had bestowed the gifts of wisdom, wealth and honour, turn away from Him so easily! The Lord spoke to the king angrily. "Solomon!" He thundered, striking fear into the king's heart. "You have not kept my covenant and laws as I commanded you to! I promised to establish your royal throne over Israel for ever if you lived by my laws, but you have worshipped pagan idols. I am therefore going to tear your kingdom away from you. However, for the sake of your father David, I will not make you suffer this in your lifetime. I will do it to the son who succeeds you on the throne. He will be left with only a small part of your kingdom, while one of your servants will rule over the rest."

> ❝ When Solomon was old, his wives turned away his heart after other gods. ❞

Even though Solomon was the most knowledgeable man in the world, he had no idea who the "servant" was that God was speaking of. It was a bitter pill to swallow. Instead of the kingdom he'd worked so hard to build going to his son, most of Solomon's efforts would be enjoyed by a stranger. Yet the king understood he had sinned. He had no choice but to accept the Lord's punishment and beg His forgiveness. The king realized that the period of peace, unity and prosperity he had brought to Israel was about to come to an end, all through his own fault. Despite all the efforts Solomon had made to live peacefully with his enemies, for the last years of his reign were plagued with unrest. Two rulers in particular continually raided Israel, King Hadad of Edom and King Rezon of Damascus. The king knew that it was the way things would be for Israel in the future.

### Shishak
The kings of Edom and Damascus were not the only ones to attack Israel during Solomon's reign – the Pharaoh Shishak also invaded. Shishak is the first Pharaoh to be mentioned by name in the Bible. This is a small silver pendant showing the Pharaoh, possibly worn on a necklace as jewellery.

### Burning incense
This picture shows an incense burner from the 10th century BC. Incense was commonly used during religious ceremonies, as an offering to God. The word "incense" refers both to the substance used for burning (usually a spice or gum) and to the characteristic smell that is produced.

### ❖ ABOUT THE STORY ❖
*Solomon failed God by allowing his wives to draw him away from God. Other nations worshipped many gods, and the temptation was great for the Israelites to do the same. Solomon, who loved God, foolishly allowed these other gods to be introduced into Israel.*

# The Kingdom is Divided

THERE was a high-ranking official in Solomon's government called Jeroboam, a very capable man who carried out his work quickly and efficiently. The king rewarded Jeroboam with promotion, making him minister over all the forced labour schemes in the territories that belonged to the tribe of Joseph.

Jeroboam was delighted. He immediately packed up his house and belongings, and set off out of Jerusalem to move to his new job. However, he hadn't long been on the road when he saw the prophet Ahijah coming towards him. To Jeroboam's astonishment, the prophet stripped off the new robe he was wearing and ripped it into twelve pieces. "I am here with a message for you from the Lord," Ahijah declared. "God is about to tear the kingdom away from Solomon and rip Israel apart, for the king has forsaken Him and turned to worshipping false idols. Solomon's son will rule over only two of the tribes, and the Lord will make you king over the other ten.'

Jeroboam was amazed. Though he was an ambitious man, he had never dreamed of being on the throne of Israel. How on earth was all of this going to happen, he wondered? He was an important man in the kingdom, but surely he wasn't important enough to be king.

Jeroboam knew that the dramatic prophecy was best kept to himself, but he couldn't resist confiding in his family and friends. They found it hard to keep the exciting

secret, and the news leaked out until people all over the country were whispering the rumour. Soon word reached the ears of the king himself. Solomon realized with dread that Jeroboam was the "servant" God had chosen to take over the kingdom. In desperation, the king sent men to kill Jeroboam, but he managed to escape and fled to the distant country of Egypt.

Finally, after reigning over Israel for forty years, King Solomon died and his son Rehoboam took the throne. Even though Solomon had made Israel a wealthy, famous country, life under him had been terribly hard. The exhausted people wanted to make sure that their new ruler would be less demanding than his father had been. They searched for a spokesperson to approach the new king, and there was no one more suitable than Jeroboam, who had returned from Egypt after Solomon died.

Rehoboam asked his counsellors what they thought he should do about the peoples' request. First he went to the advisors who used to be at his father's side. These old men knew how the people had suffered under Solomon's rule. They wisely advised the king to win the favour of his new subjects by showing them mercy and reducing the levels of taxation and forced labour.

Then Solomon's son went to his new advisers. They were inexperienced and counselled the king to show the people his authority by imposing laws that were even harsher than those of his father.

> 66 'My father chastised you with whips, but I will chastise you with scorpions.' 99

The king thought for a while. Rehoboam was an arrogant young man who liked the idea of his subjects cowering in fear before him. He foolishly chose the advice of the younger men over that of his father's more experienced counsellors and advisers. "You have asked me to lighten your yoke," he announced to the anxiously waiting people. "Hear this. My father lashed you with whips, but I am going to lash you with scorpions!"

The tyrant had expected the Israelites to shut up and meekly shuffle away at this cruel threat. He was shocked to find that it had quite the opposite effect. Labourers all over the country downed tools and sat at home, refusing to work. On top of this general strike, there were demonstrations and organized protests. Several protests broke out into violent scuffles with the king's men, who had been sent to keep the rioting workers under control. In one demonstration the king's minister in charge of Israel's forced labour, Adoram, was stoned to death. "We will no longer serve the house of David," the people shouted. "We want a new king!" The ten tribes in the north of Israel crowned Jeroboam as their new ruler.

Only the tribe of Judah and the tiny tribe of Benjamin, in the south of the country, remained faithful to Solomon's son. From them he gathered 180,000 warriors to go and fight Jeroboam for the throne. A prophet called Shemaiah stopped him, bringing word from God. "The Lord says that no one shall fight against his countrymen. Everyone must return home, for this division in the kingdom has been brought about by the Lord himself."

So the kingdom that David had unified, and that Solomon had spent years building up, was once again split into two. The ten tribes of the north kept the name Israel, and the two small tribes of the south were called Judah.

### The divided kingdom

God punished Israel heavily for Solomon's disobedience. The two new kings ruled their separate tribes. Judah and Benjamin followed Solomon's son, Rehoboam, and all the other tribes crowned Jeroboam as their new king. Two kings were not as strong as one king would have been, and they lost land to the surrounding tribes.

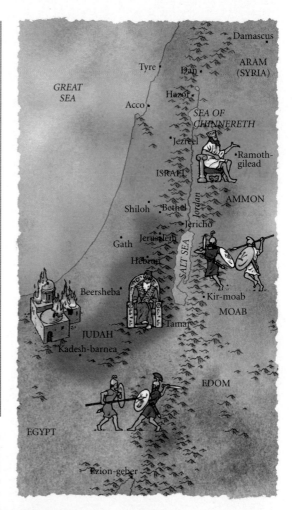

### Jeroboam's seal

In around 930BC Jeroboam became the first king of the separate Israel. The son of a wealthy landowner, he worked his way up in the royal court until he was in charge of many of Solomon's building projects. During one of these projects, Jeroboam led the workforce in a rebellion against the king's heavy-handed practices. Because of this, he was banished to Egypt, where he remained until Solomon's death. The picture shows Jeroboam's seal.

### ❖ ABOUT THE STORY ❖

*This story marks the start of 200 years of feuding between Israel in the north and Judah in the south. The division occurred in 930BC, and the tribes were never re-united. Israel was destroyed in 722BC, and Judah in 587BC, but some Jews remained to pave the way for the New Testament.*

# The Book of Proverbs

FROM earliest times there were people in Israel and across the ancient world who studied what was called "wisdom". The writers of the *Book of Proverbs* and other wisdom literature in the *Old Testament*, such as the books of Job and Ecclesiastes, discussed such difficult questions as: What is the purpose of life and why is there death, suffering and evil in the world? Some of these reflections on life are collected in the *Book of Proverbs*.

Proverbs are short sayings that are easy to remember and which teach something about life and how people should live. They are general sayings, which means that they mean something to everyone and are relevant to all people in many situations. There are proverbs in many cultures all over the world.

Many of the wise sayings in *Proverbs* are basic common sense, but they are underpinned by the belief that wisdom comes from God:

"Trust in the Lord with all your heart and lean not upon your own understanding." (3:5–6)

**Wisdom in Proverbs**
The writers give a vivid picture of wisdom:
"Length of days is in her right hand, and in her left are riches and honour. Her ways are ways of pleasantness and all her paths are peace. She is a tree of life to them that lay hold upon her, and happy is everyone that retaineth her."

WISDOM

The structure of the *Book of Proverbs* varies. Sometimes several proverbs are linked by a single theme, such as the family or laziness.

Here are some examples of wise sayings from the *Book of Proverbs*:

> *Let not loyalty and faithfulness forsake you.*
> (3:3)

> *He who seeks good finds goodwill, but evil comes to him who searches for it.*
> (11:27)

> *Even in laughter the heart is sad, and the end of joy is grief.*
> (14:13)

> *A soft answer turneth away wrath, but a harsh word stirs up anger.*
> (15:1)

> *Better a meal of vegetables where there is love than a fattened calf with hatred.*
> (15:17)

> *Pride goes before destruction and a haughty spirit before a fall.*
> (18:18)

> *Train up a child in the way he should go and when he is old he will not depart from it.*
> (22:6)

**"** *A word fitly spoken is like apples of gold in a setting of silver.* **"**
(25.11)

**"** *Like cold water to a thirsty soul, so is good news from a far country.* **"**
(25:25)

**"** *Do not boast about tomorrow for you do not know what a day may bring forth.* **"**
(27:1)

**"** *As water reflects a face, so a man's heart reflects the man.* **"**
(27:19)

## SOLOMON AND THE *BOOK OF PROVERBS*

It is generally agreed that the *Book of Proverbs* was compiled during the days of Israel's first kings, although editing continued for some centuries after this.

**"** *Let another praise you, and not your own mouth* **"**
(27:2)

It is not known exactly what Solomon's role was, but the book is introduced as 'The proverbs of Solomon, the son of David'. His name appears again at the beginning of chapters 10 and 25, and the collections of proverbs from 10:1 – 22:16 and 25:1 – 29:27 are usually attributed to him. Solomon was famous throughout the ancient world for his outstanding wisdom. Unlike the kings before and after him, he was wealthy, he had many international contacts and he was not engaged in warfare. He was able to collect and compose thousands of proverbs and songs. His court became an international centre for the exchange of learning.

---

### ✦ THEMES IN PROVERBS ✦

The themes dealt with in the *Book of Proverbs* cover all aspects of life, including home, work, relationships, justice, attitudes and everything people do, say or even think. The sayings are based on practical observations of everyday life, and there is an underlying belief behind all the proverbs that wisdom comes from God.

#### The wise man and the fool
This is the main theme of the whole book and forms the subject of the first nine chapters. The proverbs highlight the contrast between the wisdom of obeying God and the folly of wilfully going one's own way.

#### The righteous and the wicked
The wise person will lead a good, or righteous, life, whereas the fool will always be tempted by wrongdoing – in other words, he will become wicked. God loves and protects righteous people and is angry with those who are wicked. Although they may succeed for a while, it is only a matter of time before they arrive at death and destruction.

#### Laziness and hard work
Many of the proverbs describe the downfall of the lazy person. These people only realize their error too late, when they have achieved neither wealth nor status.

#### The family
This theme covers marriage, including unfaithfulness. It also covers the relationship between parents and children, including how they should be disciplined. Many of the sayings on this theme are still relevant today.

# The Temple

ALTHOUGH it was King David's great ambition to build a temple, his son, Solomon, actually ordered the work to be done. Solomon built the temple in Jerusalem as a permanent home for the Ark of the Covenant – the wooden chest containing the Ten Commandments. The temple took seven years to complete. It was built as a house for God, rather than as a place to hold big gatherings of people. We have a good idea of what it looked like because there are detailed descriptions in the Bible. Solomon may have based his temple on the temples of the pagan tribes of the time. Ruins of these have been excavated that are similar in style to the Bible descriptions.

Solomon's temple was a rectangular building. It was about 30m long, 10m wide and 15m high. The temple probably stood on a platform above the level of the courtyard in which it was built, and was reached by a flight of steps. In the courtyard, in front of the temple, was a huge bronze altar for sacrifices and an enormous bronze basin supported by twelve bronze bulls, which was used for ritual washings. There were store rooms along three sides of the building, which were probably used to keep sacred objects. The front entrance porch had a doorway with a giant bronze pillar on each side. These pillars were called Jachin and Boaz. It is not known what purpose they served as they were not part of the structure of the temple.

A pair of folding wooden doors led from the entrance porch to the outer chamber of the temple, which was known as the Holy Place. This was the larger chamber where the high priest performed ceremonial duties. The chamber was lit by five pairs of golden lampstands, and by a row of latticed windows high in the walls on each side.

A second pair of wooden doors led from the Holy Place to the inner chamber, which was known as Holy of Holies. This was a very sacred place. The doors

**Solomon's temple**
This picture shows the finished temple. In th Holy of Holies, the t guardian cherubim can be seen, their outstretched wings meeting above the Ark of the Covenan

---

TIMELINE 1100BC TO 900BC

• Eli is Judge of Israel and High Priest in the tabernacle

• Samuel is born. He works in the tabernacle with Eli, before becoming a Judge himself

1100BC

MENORAH, A SACRED LAMPSTAND

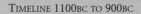

SAMUEL RECEIVING THE CALL FROM GOD

• Saul is made king by Samuel

SAMUEL ANOINTING SAUL

• David flees from Saul

• Saul is killed at the Battle of Gilboa

1050BC

• David is made king of Judah

• David is made king of all Israel

THE DEATH OF SAUL AT GILBOA

100

to it were probably only opened once a year, for the high priest at the atonement ceremony. The Ark of the Covenant lay in the Holy of Holies, guarded by two wooden cherubim, each about 5m tall. When the ark was first put in place, the Holy of Holies was filled with a cloud, which signified the presence of God.

Both the Holy Place and the Holy of Holies had walls panelled with cedarwood and floors covered with cypress planks. The walls and doors were carved with flowers, palm trees and cherubim, and inset with gold. None of the underlying stonework was visible at all.

Solomon was assisted by neighbouring tribes in the building of the temple. He already had a friendship with King Hiram of Tyre, in Phoenicia. This alliance was strengthened by the agreement that Hiram would supply many of the materials for the temple, in particular the wood, and would take charge of the building work. In return for this, Solomon would provide him with foodstuffs, such as wheat, barley and oil.

### Ancient cherubim
The figure shown on the right is actually what the cherubim in Solomon's temple would have looked like. Today we think of cherubim as looking like little children, but this figure has more in common with an Egyptian sphinx.

### The tabernacle
The tabernacle was built during the Israelites' wilderness years, as a home for the Ark of the Covenant. It was a portable temple, which could be carried wherever they went. After the Israelites settled in Canaan, the tabernacle was kept at Shiloh, Nob and Gibeon, before Solomon built his temple, and the ark was transferred there.

The skill of many craftsmen, including stonemasons, carpenters and bronze-workers, was used to build the temple. Stonemasons sawed, hammered and chiselled stone blocks into shape, to make the basic structure. The blocks were worked on before being brought to the holy site so that no unneccessary noise was made. Even during the building stage, the place was regarded as holy. Ordinary woodwork was done by carpenters, but the woodcarving, such as the cherubim and the panelling on walls and doors, was carried out by specially skilled craftsmen. For the basic woodwork, local woods, such as cedar, cypress, oak, ash and acacia, were used, but for the carving work, hard woods, such as ebony, sandalwood and boxwood, were imported from abroad. King Hiram supervised much of the bronze casting himself, including the two decorative pillars for the entrance to the temple, and the huge basin, which was able to hold nearly 45,000 litres of water.

DAVID IS MADE KING

• Death of King David

• Solomon is made king of the united kingdom of Israel

DAVID AND NATHAN

• Solomon is blessed with wisdom by God

• The Queen of Sheba visits Solomon

• Death of King Solomon

• Solomon's son, Rehoboam becomes King of Judah

WEALTH OF SOLOMON

950BC

ASSYRIAN LION'S HEAD

• Jeroboam, Solomon's servant, becomes king of Israel

• The prophet Shemaiah tells Rehoboam he must not try to invade Israel

900BC

# Glossary

**Baal**

Baal is the main god of the Canaanites, the original inhabitants of the Promised Land. He was a fertility god, the people believed that he made the crops grow for them. He was also a thunder god, and he is often pictured holding or throwing a bolt of lightning.

**Commandments**

The Ten Commandments were the most important of the laws that God gave to Moses on Mount Sinai. They are addressed to the whole of the Israelite nation, and to everyone as an individual. They were the terms of the covenant between God and his people and were produced on two stone tablets. The tablets were kept in the Ark of the Covenant.

**covenant**

A promise where God enters into a special relationship with His people. He promised His protection and the land of Canaan to Abraham and his descendants if they would be faithful to him. This idea is summed up by the prophet Jeremiah; "I will be their God, and they will be my people." The main covenants in the Old Testament are with Abraham and Moses. In the New Testament, the main covenant is with all God's people, sealed with the death of Jesus on the cross.

**Exile**

This is a very important period in Jewish history. When Israel and Judah were conquered, the Israelites living there were sent from the Promised Land to live in Babylon. It was while they were living in exile that prophets such as Ezekiel were able to bring the nation together to worship God properly.

**Exodus**

This is the name given to the journey that the Israelites made from Egypt to the promised land. "Exodus" itself means "going out", which describes how the Israelites left Egypt.

**faith**

A complete trust and unquestioning belief in something or someone. Followers of God are devoted in such a way that they will do anything that is asked of them; believing that if God has requested something then it must be right.

**grace**

The "grace" of God is the fact that God loves all the men and women that he created even though no one on earth is completely without sin.

**idol**

An idol is a statue of a person, god or animal. Idolatry is worshipping the statue, which is forbidden to the Israelites in the Ten Commandments. The Israelites often forgot or ignored this rule, and has to be reminded not to worship idols by prophets from God.

**Israel**

This was originally the nation that descended from Jacob, who was renamed Israel after wrestling all night with an angel by the river Jabbok. The new name, which means "he who has wrestled with the Lord", was a sign that God was still with him. To punish King Solomon for disobeying Him, God split Israel into two kingdoms. Solomon's son, Rehoboam, ruled over the southern part, called Judah, while Jeroboam ruled the northern part which kept the name Israel. Jeroboam set up a new capital for Israel at Samaria. Israel was conquered by the Assyrians, and its people sent away. The capital, Samaria, was occupied by people from other countries, who became known as Samaritans.

**Jew**

This was the name given to the Israelites while they were in Exile in Babylon. It was originally used to mean people from Judah, but after the Exile it came to mean people who followed the Jewish faith.

**Judah**

This is the southern part of the divided kingdom. To punish King Solomon for disobeying Him, God split Solomon's kingdom into two. Solomon's son, Rehoboam, ruled over the southern part, called Judah, while Jeroboam ruled the northern part which kept the name Israel. The capital of Judah was Jerusalem, the holy city of the Jewish faith. When Jerusalem was captured by the Babylonians, the people were sent into exile.

**miracle**

These are mighty works, performed through the power of God. Moses himself performed miracles, the most famous of which is the parting of the Red Sea. They happen not only to show God's power to people, but they also form part of God revealing Himself to His creation, humans. The most important miracle to Christianity is the resurrection of Jesus after he was crucified.

**Promised Land**

Abraham, the ancestor of all the Israelites was promised a large area east of the Mediterranean Sea, then called the Great Sea, for his descendants. When Moses led the Exodus from Egypt, he was leading the Israelites to claim the Promised Land.

**prophet**

Prophets were men or women called by God to speak for Him and to communicate His will to the people. The prophets first emerged as a group in the time of Samuel, they would offer guidance to the Israelites and warn of troubles ahead.

**sacrifice**

An offering made to God as a way for a man to give God something that belongs to him. Only the best can be offered to God, the first born lambs, or the best wheat. Sacrifices are not a person's attempt to earn favour from God, but a way to make peace with Him.

# Index